Peak Performance for Deans and Chairs

Other selected titles in the series:

Searching for Higher Education Leadership: Advice for Candidates and Search Committees
  by Jean A. Dowdall

Presidential Transitions: It's Not Just the Position, It's the Transition
  by Patrick H. Sanaghan, Larry Goldstein, and Kathleen D. Gaval

Other Duties as Assigned: Presidential Assistants in Higher Education
  by Mark P. Curchack

Changing Course: Making the Hard Decisions to Eliminate Academic Programs, Second Edition
  by Peter D. Eckel

The "How To" Grants Manual: Successful Grantseeking Techniques for Obtaining Public and Private Grants, Sixth Edition
  by David G. Bauer

International Students: Strengthening a Critical Resource
  by Maureen Andrade and Norman Evans

Leaders in the Crossroads: Success and Failure in the College Presidency
  by Stephen J. Nelson

Leading America's Branch Campuses
  edited by Samuel Schuman

Faculty Success through Mentoring: A Guide for Mentors, Mentees, and Leaders
  by Carole J. Bland, Anne L. Taylor, S. Lynn Shollen, Anne Marie Weber-Main, Patricia A. Mulcahy

Community Colleges on the Horizon: Challenge, Choice, or Abundance
  edited by Richard Alfred, Christopher Shults, Ozan Jaquette, and Shelley Strickland

Out in Front: The College President as the Face of the Institution
  edited by Lawrence V. Weill

Beyond 2020: Envisioning the Future of Universities in America
  by Mary Landon Darden

Minding the Dream: The Process and Practice of the American Community College
  by Gail O. Mellow and Cynthia Heelan

Higher Education in the Internet Age: Libraries Creating a Strategic Edge
  by Patricia Senn Breivik and E. Gordon Gee

American Places: In Search of the Twenty-First Century Campus
  by M. Perry Chapman

New Game Plan for College Sport
  edited by Richard E. Lapchick

What's Happening to Public Higher Education?
  edited by Ronald G. Ehrenberg

Lessons from the Edge: For-Profit and Nontraditional Higher Education in America
  by Gary A. Berg

Mission and Place: Strengthening Learning and Community through Campus Design
  By Daniel R. Kenney, Ricardo Dumont, and Ginger S. Kenney

Peak Performance for Deans and Chairs

Reframing Higher Education's Middle

Susan Stavert Roper and Terrence E. Deal

AMERICAN COUNCIL ON EDUCATION
® The Unifying Voice for Higher Education

ROWMAN & LITTLEFIELD EDUCATION

A division of

ROWMAN & LITTLEFIELD PUBLISHERS, INC.
Lanham • New York • Toronto • Plymouth, UK

Published in partnership with the American Council on Education

Published by Rowman & Littlefield Education
A division of Rowman & Littlefield Publishers, Inc.
A wholly owned subsidiary of The Rowman & Littlefield Publishing Group, Inc.
4501 Forbes Boulevard, Suite 200, Lanham, Maryland 20706
http://www.rowmaneducation.com

Estover Road
Plymouth PL6 7PY
United Kingdom

British Library Cataloguing in Publication Information Available

Library of Congress Cataloging-in-Publication Data

Roper, Susan Stavert.
  Peak performance for deans and chairs : reframing higher education's middle / Susan Stavert Roper and Terrence E. Deal.
     p. cm.
  Includes bibliographical references.
  ISBN 978-1-60709-536-1 (cloth : alk. paper) — ISBN 978-1-60709-538-5 (electronic)
  1. Deans (Education) 2. College department heads. 3. Universities and colleges—Administration. 4. University cooperation. 5. Total quality management in higher education. I. Deal, Terrence E. II. Title.
  LB2341.R587 2010
  378.1'11—dc22   2009031905

Printed in the United States of America

⊗™ The paper used in this publication meets the minimum requirements of American National Standard for Information Sciences—Permanence of Paper for Printed Library Materials, ANSI/NISO Z39.48-1992.

In Memory of Elizabeth G. Cohen
Our Mentor, Our Colleague, Our Friend
A superb teacher and a gifted researcher, Liz taught
us how to apply sociology to improve the quality of
education in our schools and universities. She was a
powerful influence in our lives, and we will always
love her for the gifts she gave us.

Contents

Acknowledgments

We are indebted to all the department chairs and deans who not only educated us but also honored us with their trust. The personal accounts of their struggles and successes broadened and deepened our understanding. Colleagues from the American Association of Colleges for Teacher Education (AACTE) have been particularly generous. They include: Dolores Escobar, Gary Fenstermacher, Allen Glenn, Irma Guzman-Wagner, Randy Hitz, Richard Kunkel, Tom Lasley, Steve Lilly, Geoff Mills, Richard Schwab, Jill Tarule, and Arthurlene Towner.

We are especially grateful to the "founding fathers" of AACTE's New Dean's Institute: Jack Gant, David Imig, and David Smith. Their insights are interwoven throughout the book. Closer to home, we would like to thank our Cal Poly colleagues Phillip Bailey and Susan Opava for inspiring two of our scenarios. For their stimulating ideas and constructive criticism we thank current and former deans and chairs in the California State University system including: Andrea Brown, Carl Brown, Elaine Chin, Phyllis Fernlund, Harry Hellenbrand, Bonnie Konopak, and Paul Zingg. A special thank you to Jim Fouche who helped shape the early drafts of our manuscript. We would also like to acknowledge Lee G. Bolman, the co-creator (along with Deal) of the "reframing" approach. Although he was not involved directly in writing this manuscript, we are grateful to Lee for his unofficial influence throughout the book.

For preparing the manuscript for publication, we owe Dianne Ellis a huge debt. Susan Slesinger and Paula Moore of the American Council on Education could not have been more helpful and supportive. Patti Belcher patiently walked us through Rowman & Littlefield's guidelines. Without the encouragement and assistance of these good people, we would not have made the jump from a rough manuscript to a finished book. Despite our extended periods of procrastination, our friends Susan Bradley, Dave and Sabra Hoffman, Pat Iwata, and Diane Schaffer never wavered in their faith that one day we would complete the book.

Our families provided more than the usual support and love—without which writing would be dreary, if not impossible. Nancy Lindsay enlarged our conception of symbolic leadership by sharing her experiences as a human resources manager at Intel and tutored her technologically challenged sister. Richard Roper revealed the frustrations of young faculty members and shared foibles common to music departments. Dwight Roper's contributions over the past forty years have become so integrated into our thinking that we are no longer able to thank him for all the ways the book and our lives have gained from his wisdom. Still, we hope he knows how much we relied on his experiences as a university administrator and professor, boundless intellectual curiosity, advanced "crap detection" skills, and unstinting devotion. Sandy Deal's psychological training enables her to approach the field of organizations with a distinctive and illuminating slant. Sandy performed far beyond the call of matrimony as the Florence Nightingale of San Luis Obispo, helping Terry transcend the assorted health hurdles that waylaid him during the writing. Her love and support over the long run have made all the difference.

Chapter 1

Introduction

Trapped between a Rock and a Hard Place

These are not the best of times for institutions of higher education. Resources are scarce. Squabbles among administrators, faculty, and students are legendary. Even alumni are restive and not at all bashful about making demands public. One jaundiced college president lamented that his main job seemed to be providing employment and parking for the faculty, football for the alumni, and sex for the students (Bolman and Deal, 2003, p. 196).

The president is not alone in his misery. Colleges and universities are complex, paradoxical organizations. They are supposed to open new vistas, but mostly exist to bestow higher status. They are charged with generating useful new knowledge, but reward faculty mainly for publishing work in esoteric academic journals-or perish. They champion shared governance, but it is typically unclear who has final authority over decisions. Because of all this, institutions of higher education have been labeled as "organized anarchies" (March and Olsen, 1976).

For deans and department chairs, this conjures up a pot full of trouble. They are caught between a rock and a hard place. They are squeezed between the provost and president, at whose pleasure they serve, and faculty in their respective colleges and departments who can make life pretty miserable. As the late Arthur Coladarci, former dean of Stanford's School of Education, once quipped: "A dean is to the faculty as a fire hydrant is to a pack of dogs" (overheard by authors in the Cubberly School of Education building at Stanford).

If you step back and think about it, deans and chairs are the key linchpins that connect the institution's mission with the faculty's teaching and research. But their authority is limited and their power constrained. Because of this they must rely heavily on relationships and an accurate read of everyday situations

1

to get anything done. Amidst a tangled web of interests, voices, and issues, they must cut through the complexity to grasp what is really important.

Our aim is to help deans and department chairs (present and future) find better ways to escape the snare. To do this, we have drawn on the approach of *Reframing Organizations* (2003). We selected this approach because it presents multiple lenses for sorting through complex messes. This flexibility gives leaders a comprehensive picture of what is really going on and realistic options for what they might do. In the Air Force, this is called "situational analysis," the ability to size up knotty circumstances quickly and respond in kind. The problem is that many, if not most, deans and chairs are limited in their perspective to capture the real issues in their colleges and departments. As a result, their responses often make things worse instead of better.

Admiral Carlisle Trost, former Chief of Naval Operations, offered a way out of the trap when he remarked that the first requirement of a good leader is the ability to "figure out what's going on" (Trost, 1989). For deans and chairs, this means developing the cognitive flexibility to look at their organizations through multiple frames or lenses. Bolman and Deal (2003) offer four:

- The human resource frame emphasizes individuals and their needs. An effective organization creates a caring, trusting environment where people can learn and grow. Without such personal support, people rebel, withdraw, or get even.
- The structural frame stresses clarity and results. In organizations, people are assigned to roles and held accountable for getting the job done efficiently. Plans, policies, rules, and formal meetings coordinate efforts. A chain of command gives some individuals authority over others. Top performance is the result of a rationally designed structure equal to everyday challenges.
- The political perspective sees authority as only one form of power. Authority is assigned; power is up for grabs. Individuals and groups use power to advance special interests rather than to attain formal goals. The result is conflict, which the political lens accepts as a normal by-product of collective best resolved through compromise and bargaining.
- The symbolic frame accentuates the central role symbols play in life. Work needs meaning and purpose as much as its practical outcome of providing a paycheck. Organizations are tribal creations where a shared culture is expressed through history, values, rituals, ceremonies, sagas, and stories. An informal network of heroes and heroines, priests, storytellers, gossips, and spies determine how people behave and how well the enterprise performs. An effective organization relies heavily on hope, faith, and shared purpose.

Although the frames overlap at times, their differences are profound. As illustrated in Table 1.1, each reveals different assumptions, unique views of leadership, and novel takes on leadership challenges. Looking through all four frames provides a deeper understanding of the dynamics under the commonly accepted veneer. The frames not only enhance analysis of a problem but also suggest strategies for moving forward. In describing frames, we deliberately mix metaphors, referring to them as lenses, perspectives, windows, maps, and orientations because all of those images capture part of the idea we want to convey (Bolman and Deal, 2003, p. 12).

The problem is that most leaders scrutinize situations through only one or, at most, two lenses, limiting the strategies they employ. Favorites of most department chairs and deans are the structural and human resources perspectives, although most problems they wrestle with are political and symbolic. As a result, too much energy is expended working on the wrong things. Very few deans or chairs report having time on their hands; most are buried with too much to do. This book will help aspiring, as well as seated deans and chairs, to become aware of their strengths and limitations. By acquiring new and more powerful tools, they can learn to reframe the daunting challenges they face and achieve peak performance.

Table 1.1. Overview of the Four-Frame Model

	FRAMES			
	Structural	*Human resources*	*Political*	*Symbolic*
Metaphor for organization	Factory or machine	Family	Jungle	Carnival, temple, theatre
Central concepts	Rules, roles, goals, policies, technology, environment	Needs, skills, relationships	Power, conflict, competition, organizational politics	Culture, meaning, metaphor, ritual, ceremony, stories, heroes
Image of leadership	Social architecture	Empowerment	Advocacy	Inspiration
Basic leadership challenge	Attune structure to task, technology, environment	Align organizational and human needs	Develop agenda and power base	Create faith, beauty, and meaning

Source: Bolman and Deal (2003), p. 16. Table 2.1

Ours is not a psychological quest. We do not concentrate on personality characteristics of academic leaders. We are convinced that personalities of leaders vary as much as they do in the general population. Leadership depends as much upon context as it does on the individual. It is the leader's ability to read and respond to the demands of the circumstance we see as crucial. We present a more multi-disciplinary perspective with a focus on the organization—the university, and particularly its colleges and departments.

While we tried to choose scenarios germane across a broad cross-section of deans and department chairs, we are aware that the institution's context as well as the leader's characteristics makes a difference. Contextual factors include, among others: the size, mission and status of the institution; whether the university is private or public; whether it primarily serves graduate students or undergraduates; the relative importance of teaching versus research; and the special mission or distinctive character of the university. Moreover, these factors often intermingle to make their influence even greater.

We wanted to speak to deans and chairs directly but realize that readers will need to adjust our observations to make them applicable to their situations. We have included representative department chairs and deans from the broad range of public and private universities in the United States rather than from a few elite institutions. Some of our leaders are new to their jobs and others have considerable experience. We varied the colleges, departments, and characteristics of the leaders to incorporate some of the contextual and leadership variables we think most salient.

In our descriptions of organizational frames we paint realistic pictures of deans and department chairs struggling with common problems. In Chapter 2, three academic leaders who failed to accomplish their goals describe "the way it is." Two of the leaders are deans and one is a department chair. We use the frames as conceptual tools to examine these leaders' actions and the reactions of faculty members and others. Within each frame we suggest alternative actions the dean and chair could have taken that may have been more effective

In Chapters 3, 4, 5, and 6, we present both negative and positive scenarios of deans and chairs. We analyze each scenario by applying all the frames to enhance understanding of the academic setting and to suggest a greater range of potential actions. We highlight "Lessons Learned" in *italics*. The scenarios and subsequent analysis are related to common issues that deans and chairs face. In Chapter 3, deans struggle to avoid bedlam and tame turbulence as they try to implement change. In Chapter 4, department chairs confront "creeps" and "cliques" in their efforts to lead faculty. Surviving financial cutbacks is the focus of Chapter 5. We compare a dean who leads his college through the fiscal crisis with a dean who is caught flat-footed when the budget must be trimmed. In Chapter 6, we focus on the relationships with "higher-ups," particularly with the provost, a university's chief academic officer and a dean's immediate superior. Chapter 7 describes "the way it's 'spozed to be" by showing how multiple lenses can help a new dean or department chair create options for dealing better with vexations and tribulations. We wrap it all up in Chapter 8 where we conclude with a summary, advice to practice, practice, practice and gain the courage to persevere.

Throughout the book, our key medium is stories. In recent memory, for some reason, stories got a bad name. Professors who relied on examples and narrative were accused of telling "war stories"—not seen as a positive pedagogical strategy. But current writings and research have resurrected the story as one of the most powerful ways we acquire the valuable lessons of leadership. We learn from our triumphs and those of others. We learn even more from our own tragedies and mistakes. When a Southwest Airline's executive launched an expensive new initiative, it flopped—big time. Southwest's CEO Herb Kelleher summoned him to his office for what the executive believed would be his last day with the company. He was pleasantly surprised. Kelleher promoted the executive telling him: "That was such a big error you must have learned a lot" (personal communication with authors). In the next chapter, we present three classic failures, using the four frames to tease out some fundamental lessons of avoiding pitfalls and determining what's next when things go wrong.

Chapter 2

The Way It Is

Ferreting Out Root Stresses and Plotting New Tactics

WELL-INTENDED STRATEGIES BACKFIRE

Very often, the only safe haven for university deans and department chairs is at an annual conference with their peers. Embattled administrators gather to soothe their wounds and summon the spirit that will allow them to survive another year. Quite typically, those who want to crow about their triumphs dominate in formal sessions. Those who are less lucky, or more honest, spend more time hanging out with their colleagues in bars and sponsored social hours. There they can drop their guard and talk truth. The venting helps but rarely is any headway made on what to do with vexing troubles. The same issues resurface every year with very little notable progress.

After a particularly trying day at an academic leadership conference, three attendees gathered for dinner to grouse about their meetings. "The thing I hate most about these sessions," Richard Rogers observed, "is that they are like the 'bring and brag' sessions in kindergarten. People break their arms patting themselves on the back. Isn't anyone but me wrestling with an endless barrage of hairy problems?"

"I know what you mean," replied Julie. "Higher education is getting trounced. We're all continually told to 'do more with less,' yet we still play the one-ups-man game of 'Who's the best dean?' With all the stuff that's staring me in the face, I just can't fake it any more."

Dara chimed in. "You're not alone. The sessions for department chairs are just as frustrating. We only hear about the good things going on. I'm so pissed-off with my faculty that I'm ready to resign. But if I shared my sad story in a meeting here I'd probably be snubbed and never get another job."

Richard responded empathically, "Hey, I have an idea. Why don't we all cough up our worst story? I'd love a sympathetic audience to share the grief. Julie, instead of faking it, here's a chance to let your hair down."

DEAN JULIE BAXTER'S STORY

"For openers, here's a lesson in what not to do. I've spent a good share of my life over the past couple of years trying to increase alumni giving. That's an uphill battle in a College of Liberal Arts because most of our graduates don't end up wealthy enough to make major donations. In fact, I see all too many of them waiting tables in our local restaurants. Thanks to our Advancement Office though, I was able to identify a few prospects. I really worked hard to cultivate them. I invited them to dinner at my house, took them on tours of our college, introduced them to students and faculty members, and spent many hours listening to their concerns and interests.

"This summer I finally hit it big. One of my prospects, a guy who switched from teaching English to real estate and made a bundle in the good old days, said he thought we needed a new recital hall. Turns out, his wife was a dancer and they've been disappointed that we have no decent venue for our dance majors to perform. Now, I'll admit I would have been happier if he had been interested in funding scholarships or endowing a faculty position, but after all, it's his money. I immediately got the ball rolling with the facilities-planning people. I promised him we'd name the hall after him and his wife.

"As you can imagine, the president was happy as a clam. I sure wish I could say the same about my faculty. The only one who was positive was the dance instructor and she's a non-tenure track lecturer. I got openly attacked in a faculty meeting and nobody came to my defense. They accused me of ignoring their needs and spending too much time off campus with 'rich, white men.' When I thought of all the weekends and evenings I spent trying to bring in more money for our college, I was furious. I let them know that they were not my supervisors. I told them that as the leader of this college, I consider faculty and student input, but I determine my priorities in consultation with the provost and president. I didn't say 'if you don't like it, lump it,' but that's what I was thinking and probably projecting. That was a month ago and now I hear that some faculty members are proposing a vote of 'no confidence' in me. I can hardly believe it after all I've done for this college. Where did I go wrong?"

DEAN RICHARD ROGERS' STORY

"Faculty members can be cruel and ungrateful. Give them a handout and they bite off your hand. Since misery loves company, I'll share a similar experience. I was under the usual time crunch. Our State Board of Higher Education, in their infinite wisdom, decided that all public campuses should switch from the quarter calendar to an early semester calendar. They gave us only one academic year to revise our programs. We're a big college in a big university. I knew that we had to pull together if we were to meet the deadline. Being a cockeyed optimist, I saw the mandated change as an opportunity to make other improvements that were long overdue.

"I told my department chairs that this was a chance to improve programs, eliminate repetition in our current courses, and integrate technology across the curriculum. I got some dirty looks when I recommended we eliminate senior faculty 'ownership' of classes and give newer faculty a chance to teach some of them. I suggested we agree on common themes and broad goals to guide our revisions. But as both of you know, revising curriculum is a departmental responsibility so I delegated the task to department chairs. I told them I'd be happy to meet with their departments to more fully explain my ideas. No one asked.

"To make a long story short, we met the one-year deadline but changes were minimal and superficial. Faculty members exerted little effort. The chairs did a poor job of motivating and organizing them. I'm really disappointed in all of us but I haven't a clue on what I could have done differently."

CHAIR DARA HEADLY'S STORY

"Compared to your disasters, my problem sounds minor. But it is very troublesome to me. I'm chair of a Civil Engineering Department in a university known for its engineering programs. Most of my department's faculty is white males. Yet, more and more students are women and minorities.

"I agreed to become chair because I really wanted to diversify our faculty. As a former faculty member, I heartily endorsed full participation in decision-making. As chair, I gave the faculty wide latitude in recruiting and selecting new faculty members. It seems I've succeeded in delegating decision-making. Everyone has a say, except me.

"As a result, no female candidate has been hired in the five positions we've filled. We brought in a couple of males from India, but no women or candidates from underrepresented ethnic or racial groups in our own

country. I'm embarrassed because I personally recruited some strong female
and minority candidates. Search committees rejected them. At this point, my
only role in the search process is to pass along top candidates' files to the
dean. Short of organizing a protest and picketing my own department, I am
at a loss."

WHAT'S GOING ON HERE?

Were the failures of these well-intentioned leaders inevitable? We think not.
Each of them is smart enough. But their ability to read situations is limited.
They are surprised when their well-intended strategies backfire. Even in
retrospect, they appear clueless about what happened and what they might
have done differently. They are certainly not alone in failing to understand
the complexity of organizations and the demands of leadership. But lacking
multiple perspectives, they are deprived of a variety of practical options that
would help them become more effective. Let us take a look through each of
the four frames to expand our understanding of the challenges Richard, Julie,
and Dara faced and see if we can't come up with better strategies they could
have implemented.

THE STRUCTURAL PERSPECTIVE

The structural perspective is what most people use to look at organizations. The vertical structure is portrayed in organizational charts. What is
the hierarchy? Who reports to whom? What are the responsibilities of each
position? (Bolman and Deal, 2003, Table 1.1., p. 17) In the public university
system where Dean Rogers served, the State Board of Higher Education set
the policy for a new academic calendar. The chancellor's role was to carry
out the board's policies. He directed the university president to ensure its
implementation. The president delegated this job to the provost who, in turn,
assigned the task to college deans.

Richard carried on this tradition because he saw only the vertical structure,
that is, the official hierarchy of the university. He relied on his "legitimate
authority" as dean when he directed department chairs to work with faculty
members to improve their programs as they transitioned to a new calendar.
He assumed that chairs had the clout and the will to get the job done. The
structural frame reminds us, however, that the university is simultaneously hierarchical and decentralized. Both perspectives need to be considered. Richard might have learned something by reading Russo's academic

spoof, *Straight Man*. Russo's protagonist wryly observes, "There are many advantages to being the chair in an English Department, but giving orders isn't one of them. Actually you can give all the orders you want, as long as you don't mind them being ignored" (Russo, 1997, p. 233).

Like Richard, Julie seemed to understand only the formal chain of command, neglecting decentralized centers of power. Ironically, while Richard's structural perspective justified his decision to delegate, Julie used the same perspective to vindicate her unilateral decisions. Neither appreciated the unique combination of lateral and vertical communication channels that characterize university structure. Faculty members believe that they should have the major voice in setting university policies, whether or not administrators agree with them. Although we all have heard faculty members persistently complain abut the excessive time they devote to committee work, few see directives from deans or chairs as an improvement. Woe to the administrator who fails to understand this. Time pressures, like those Julie and Richard faced, often cause administrators to overlook the amorphous nature of how things really do or don't get done.

Henry Rosovsky, former dean of Arts and Sciences at Harvard University, notes, "the critical feature of 'academic life' is the absence of a boss" (Rosovsky, 1990, p. 163). Dara was all too eager to agree with Rosovsky. Unlike Julie and Richard, Dara did not see herself in the formal hierarchy. In Dara's view, only the university's decentralized structure, with its emphasis on faculty governance, was significant. In her over-riding concern with full faculty participation, she neglected to define her own role in the search process.

Problems arise when the structure does not fit the situation. All three of our leaders may have benefited by learning the basic lesson of a successful commando team: "vary the structure in response to changes in task and circumstances" (Bolman and Deal, 2003, p. 109). The variety of positions, roles, rules, policies, procedures, task forces, and ad hoc committees in departments and colleges, even in the same university, is ample evidence that deans and chairs have considerable latitude in organizing how tasks get accomplished.

Let's consider just one example of how aligning the structure with the task at hand could have helped one of our fearless leaders. If Dara had appointed an affirmative action officer to serve on search committees in her department, more women and minorities probably would have been hired. The affirmative action advocate could have helped to align the structure in Dara's department with her goal of diversifying the faculty.

But structural logic doesn't tell the whole story of what happened to our three administrators. Other frames are needed to understand the complexity of what they were up against. Had Julie, Richard, and Dara reframed their problems through a human resource lens, how might their approaches have been different?

THE HUMAN RESOURCES FRAME

The key to the human resources frame is tailoring an organization to meet the needs of people. "To find a way for people to get the job done while feeling good about what they are doing" is the quest of an effective human resources leader (Bolman and Deal, 2003, p. 14). Sounds simple? It is not.

For one thing, it is common to confuse human resources leadership with behaving humanely. If leaders are courteous, civil, and friendly, they see themselves as competent in this frame. As a matter of fact, deans and department chairs are expected at a minimum to behave decorously. In his study of deans, Morris reminds us that:

> Faculty members are permitted to lose their tempers, break down in tears, call each other names, and insult the dean covertly or publicly. This license does not extend to deans, however, even under the most outrageous of provocation. Free speech applies to faculty members, not to administrators (Morris, 1981, p. 24).

There is much more than being humane to become a good human resources leader. Although we should also note here that leaders typically believe that they are a lot more humane than they appear to others. We repeatedly see a discrepancy between what deans and chairs say they do and what they actually do. Deans and chairs are not unique in this respect. According to Argyris and Schon (1974), managers typically see themselves as rational, open, concerned for others, and democratic. But their actions seem to be governed more by competition, self-protection, and the desire to control. We suspect that Julie perceived her decisions as rational and showing concern for others. Richard seemed to think he was open and democratic. Neither were competent human resources leaders.

So what does it take to be a good leader as seen through the human resources frame? Bolman and Deal (2003, pp. 165–66) identify three principles for leaders to follow.

Emphasize Common Goals and Mutual Influence in Relationships

For example, Dara might have gained more support for hiring underrepresented candidates if she had convinced faculty members that these new faculty members would help them reach their common goal of increasing student enrollment. Or Richard could have visited a few highly respected faculty members in their offices and asked them, "What improvements do you think we can make as we plan for the semester system?" At the very least, he would have communicated that he cared what these faculty members thought and he probably would have discovered that he shared some common goals with them.

Communicate Openly and Publicly Test Assumptions and Beliefs

Had Richard and Julie followed this principle, they would have learned that simply listening to a concerned faculty member, along with updating the faculty with complete and straightforward information, makes a big difference. Two-way communication promotes honest interaction and encourages faculty members to assume ownership for needed changes. When leaders publicly test their assumptions, they expose doubts about their own infallibility. That sends a clear message: it's OK to change your opinion—a valuable message from any administrator trying to make changes.

Combine Advocacy with Inquiry

For example, Julie could have launched the college's fund-raising campaign by asking faculty members to identify their funding priorities. Afterwards, she could have announced the donation for the new dance theatre as the "kick-off" contribution for the college's campaign. Had Dara presented evidence of the growing number of female and minority students applying to engineering programs to the search committees, she might have experienced the power of combining advocacy with inquiry.

Finding out what others think and being prepared to advocate for their ideas may look like a sure-fire way to lose credit for accomplishments. Not finding out what faculty members were thinking turned out to be a sure-fire way to torpedo Richard and Julie's goals. One thing is certain. If a leader is convinced that he or she cannot deal with people in a supportive and collegial manner, that leader will probably be right. The self-fulfilling prophecy is bound to constrain that leader from taking the kinds of risks needed to follow the three human resources principles. We have seen fearful deans and chairs dominate discussions of controversial issues in a vain attempt to stifle opposition. Their behavior only strengthened and intensified the opposition.

Following Bolman and Deal's (2003) three human resources principles may initially make leaders feel vulnerable. In the long run, however, that will be better than giving orders (as Richard did), giving up (as Dara was about to do), and making unilateral decisions (as Julie did). Actions consistent with the three human resources principles are ones that would be expected from a trusted colleague.

THE POLITICAL LENS

Politics also played a central role in all three situations. Too many academic administrators view power and conflict negatively and believe they should "rise above" political confrontations. The political lens takes the opposite view. Politics is inevitable in all organizations, large or small. Resources are always in short supply. Special interest groups exercise power to get their share and to have their way. Unlike authority, which is legitimate and formally allocated, other sources of power are up for grabs. People can get power through a number of ways, including personality, expertise, control of information and resources, and even coercive force (Bolman and Deal, 2003, pp 194–95). The main by-product of this constant jockeying for power is conflict. Academic leaders are especially uncomfortable in dealing with conflict. If they are unable to smooth conflict over, they try to ignore it. This can result in unleashed sabotage or no-holds-barred street fights behind the scenes (Bolman and Deal, 2003, p. 186).

A common feature of the stories in this chapter is that all three leaders avoided the political process. By trying to ignore or rise above conflict, they found that negative faculty members were delighted to step into the leadership vacuum they created. From the faculty's point of view, Dean Richard Rogers, Dean Julie Baxter, and Chair Dara Headly posed risks. Julie's unilateral decision accepting the donation of funds to build a dance studio put collegial governance at risk. Dara's commitment to increase faculty diversity threatened search committee members anxious to retain their power to select new colleagues. Richard's faculty thought his proposed changes would require them to devote substantial time and effort to transition to the new calendar, thereby putting the quality of their teaching and research at risk.

We are convinced that all of these risks were worth taking. Deans and chairs have to take risks if they are to move their units ahead. But most do not realize that the price of risk-taking is conflict. Conflict scares them. Like Dara, Julie, and Richard, they are unable to reframe challenges using a political perspective where the challenge is to learn how to manage conflict instead of avoiding it.

The lessons of the political frame are to: (1) develop an agenda; (2) gain support for the agenda; and, (3) be willing to bargain and negotiate (Bolman and Deal, 2003, pp. 205–15). These are core leadership skills. Effective leaders practice them day-in and day-out.

Julie, Richard, and Dara failed to clearly communicate their agendas and to build support networks for getting them adopted. One of the only common traits of good leaders found in the voluminous literature on leadership is that good leaders articulate a clear vision or agenda. Of course, effective leaders, especially in a collegial setting such as the university, do not formulate their vision in isolation. They listen. Effective deans listen attentively to presidents, provosts, faculty members, students, and other stakeholders. They get a preliminary reading on support for and opposition to their ideas. More important, they acquire information that helps make their agenda more compelling to those who have to implement it. Pushed by deadlines, Richard and Julie did not believe they had time to develop a "shared vision."

A basic principle of the political frame is that any agenda needs a "power base." Many deans and department chairs do not know how to build coalitions with enough clout to move things ahead. Like Richard, they believe that once they communicate their agenda, they can step aside and allow faculty members independently to climb aboard. This sentiment ignores the reality that the opposition will be busy building its own networks.

A willingness and ability to bargain and negotiate is the third general strategy from the political frame. The leaders in our stories seemed unwilling or unable to bargain. For example, what a difference it might have made if Richard had offered some bargaining chips and incentives to encourage faculty members to undertake program improvement as they revised their curriculum for the semester system. He could have begun by asking the department chairs what they thought it would take to engage faculty members in this task.

The lessons of the political frame must be learned so thoroughly because they are practiced again and again. As our three victims could no doubt tell us, "happily ever after exists only in fairy tales" (Bolman and Deal, 2003, p. 225).

THE SYMBOLIC WINDOW

The symbolic is the least understood and studied of the four frames. But, in many situations it is the most powerful. A basic assumption of the symbolic frame is: "What is most important is not what happens but what it means" (Bolman and Deal, 2003, p. 242). Secular myths, sagas, metaphors, rituals, ceremonies, heroes, humor, stories, play and organizational theatre provide the material for building a culture to provide meaning in our work lives. Burton Clark (1971) described this bundle of symbolic forms and actions as the organization's "saga" which transforms a rational organization into a "beloved institution."

At Stanford University, for example, faculty, staff, and students all hear how Stanford got its start. Leland and Jane Stanford wanted a fitting memorial for their son who died at the age of sixteen of typhoid fever in Italy. They went first to Harvard to donate a building in Leland Junior's honor. Leland and Jane and their "new money" were turned away. When they came home to

California, they built their own university. For years, a popular product in the Stanford Bookstore was a T-shirt with the inscription, "Harvard—Stanford of the East." It encapsulated Stanford's founding saga.

Stories, tales, and yarns do not have the longevity of sagas, but they are nonetheless valuable to organizations. While 'Telling Good Stories' is unlikely to be found as a topic in administrative training programs, good stories build cohesion, provide security, and even entertain. Let us pass on a story to Dara that illustrates how stories can build morale.

We know a dean who worked tirelessly to diversify the faculty. Over a period of fifteen years, the number of female and ethnic minority faculty members tripled. When the senior faculty members congratulated the dean on his success in diversifying their college's faculty, the dean looked around the room and exclaimed, "The people who really made this happen were all you white, middle-aged men. You were the ones who served on search commit-tees, recruited, and attracted such stellar candidates. You recommended that I hire your new colleagues. I just did what you told me to do."

The phrases "empty ritual" and "only ceremonial" demean the value that rituals and ceremonies can play in building a strong, positive culture in an organization. For example, had Richard reframed the challenge of transition-ing to the new calendar symbolically, he might have hosted a ceremony to launch the college's effort to kick off the move to the new semester programs. After the work was done, he could have held a celebration with awards for the departments that made the most improvements and special recognition to faculty members who were the primary "movers and shakers." We have rarely heard university faculty truthfully complain about too many celebra-tions or faculty awards.

We suspect our three leaders might have been more successful had they been less earnest and more humorous. Frederick Burk, the first president of San Francisco State, warned that, "Humor may be only the first sign of intel-ligence. But, if you don't find that first sign, don't waste time looking for any other" (personal communication with Burk's son). "Hansot (1979) argues that it is less important to ask why people use humor in organizations than to ask why they are so serious. . . . humor can establish solidarity and facilitate face saving" (Bolman and Deal, 2003, p. 268).

What if Richard had started out his faculty meeting with the question, "Hey folks, guess what the Board of Higher Education, in all its wisdom, has drummed up for us to do now?" Setting this kind of tone may have led faculty to perceive him as in their camp instead of in cahoots with the "order givers." While this example expresses skepticism, it also expresses solidarity.

Humor can defuse potentially explosive situations, as well as make people feel comfortable, welcome, and happy. When he was serving as dean of the largest school at Harvard University, Henry Rosovsky compared his job to that of a dentist: "twelve to fourteen interviews a day frequently accompanied by pain" (Rosovsky, 1990, p. 241). That quip resulted in an angry letter from an official of the dental profession's national organization, but it delighted his faculty.

Providing the opportunity to play together builds community. The social gathering at the beginning of the year is a ritual in most universities. Given the challenges their units were facing, Richard, Julie and Dara would have been wise to schedule some time for play. An informal get together, especially where there are non-shop related activities, builds a group's spirit and helps break down barriers between administrators and faculty members.

Learning about the culture, history, and values in your department or college is an important symbolic lesson. In splintered cultures, there are always multiple interpretations of what things mean and what to do about them. A quick consult with the department or college's priest or priestess will help to identify historic "land-mines" and illuminate how to approach the situation honoring deeply held cultural ways. Deans and chairs who know how to capitalize on their unit's rituals, ceremonies, and myths, celebrate its heroes, and tell good stories have a portfolio that will be the envy of their colleagues. If, in addition, they can help people see the humor in their deliberations, have fun together, and learn to laugh at themselves, they are more likely to bring out the best in their faculty and staff.

DIFFERENT LENSES CORRECT BLIND SPOTS

As we saw, Richard and Julie relied primarily on the hierarchical dimension of the structural frame. Dara relied on a lateral, or horizontal. view of the structure. Blind spots in their cognitive repertoires prevented them from seeing other options. When figuring out why people act the way they do, viewing the situation through multiple frames is helpful. Sometimes a leader will feel that a person's actions make no sense. When this happens the leader should ask, "Is this person operating from a different set of perspectives than mine?"

To make this point more concrete, let us take a look at a couple of related, common practices in university life: planning and meetings. Bolman and Deal (2003) describe the multiple purposes of both according to the four frames.

No wonder it's hard to get things done in academe. The dean is likely convinced that planning is for the sole purpose of setting goals and coordinating resources to reach those goals. At least a few faculty members, and probably the most vocal ones, see planning as an arena for airing conflict and meetings

Table 2.1. Four Interpretations of Planning and Meetings

	Structural frame	*Human resources frame*	*Political frame*	*Symbolic frame*
Planning	Creating strategies to set objectives and coordinate resources	Gatherings to promote participation	Arena to air conflict and realign power	Ritual to signal responsibility, produce symbols, negotiate meanings
Meetings	Formal occasions for making decisions	Informal occasions for involvement, sharing feelings	Competitive occasions to win points	Sacred occasions to celebrate and transform the culture

Source: Bolman and Deal, 2003, Table 15.1, p. 306–07

as a venue for competing to win points. Then, there are others who simply want to participate in a relaxed, informal setting where they can share their thoughts and feelings.

It is difficult to imagine a more divergent set of perspectives. Of course administrators are confused and often become victims. We know most managers rely primarily on the structural or human resources frames. They rarely consider political or symbolic realities.

> Led to believe that they should be rational and on top of things, managers become confused and bewildered. They are supposed to plan and organize, yet they find themselves muddling and playing catch-up. They want to solve problems and make decisions. But problems are ill-defined and options murky. Control is an illusion and rationality an afterthought. (Bolman and Deal, 2003, p. 305)

With this background in mind, we examine other situations leaders face in the university setting. In the next chapter, we look at how deans can implement long-lasting change. We start with the scenario of a dean who tried and failed to make changes in her college and compare her with a dean who succeeded. By looking through the four frames at these two deans, we identify lessons to help deans and chairs become successful change agents.

Chapter 3

Change

Stifling Bedlam and Taming Turbulence

DOUBLE-CROSSING THE DEAN

Sonia's final hurdle for the dean's position in the School of Education was an interview with the university's president. Since he did not even have a provost, Sonia knew that the president was the one she had to impress. He would do the hiring. She was aware beforehand that one of the president's top priorities was to upgrade the faculty. During the interview, as Sonia looked around the president's office, she couldn't help but notice a prominently displayed doctoral degree from Yale. It seemed a little out of place in a small, rural campus where faculty members were more likely to decorate offices with pictures of family and fishing trips than with diplomas. But then, the president was the only one on campus with a doctorate from such a prestigious university.

Sonia suspected that the president would have a specific agenda for the prospective new dean. She didn't have to wait long to find out what it was. After the president hurried into their appointment and told her how impressed he was with her vita, particularly her graduate work at the University of Michigan, he put his cards on the table.

"Sonia, I'd like to know if you are as interested in us as we are in you." When Sonia assured him that she was, he came to the point. "I've been here four years and we've made significant changes in the quality of this university by hiring excellent new faculty members. Unfortunately, we haven't been able to hire any new blood in the education school. That's all about to change. Four education professors are retiring this year. Next year, I expect another three faculty members will leave. Taking a five-year perspective, I anticipate that more than half of the faculty positions will be open. As you know, it's a comparatively small school. The new dean will hire these new faculty members, who will become the school's majority. I want them to be among the best in the country—national reputations. How does that sound?"

Sonia responded enthusiastically. "I know that I can recruit strong candidates. I'm active in several professional associations and have contacts at most of the top education schools in the country. But if I get the job, I'd need a lot of support from you to attract faculty members of this caliber. They don't come cheap."

The president smiled and assured Sonia, "You can count on me. You'll have carte blanche."

Two days later, the president offered Sonia the job. "You're our first choice. You have an open field to turn this school around. I hope you will accept our offer." Sonia jumped at the chance to take on a dean's dream job. "I can hardly wait to get started. I've been looking for a university where I can do something exciting. Although I'm in a bigger university now, my influence as department chair is pretty limited. I'm ready for this challenge!"

Sonia charged into her new assignment on the run. As a former department chair, Sonia knew that universities who recruit new faculty members early are more likely to attract a better and bigger pool of candidates. At her first faculty meeting, Sonia laid out her ambitious plans for new faculty recruitment and selection. "I've been in academic administration for six years. I know that the most important decisions I make will be our new hires. I will work with department chairs to organize search committees immediately and promise that I will do everything in my power to ensure that we bring in strong candidates. This is a rare opportunity to put our school on the map. I look forward to working with you to make it happen."

Sonia followed through right away. She directed department chairs to appoint their best faculty members to search committees. Once the committees drafted vacancy notices, Sonia made sure they all included, "evidence of scholarly potential and work," and moved the deadline for applications up a month.

Despite her busy days trying to get oriented to a new school, university, and community, Sonia charged into the recruitment effort. She personally sent vacancy notices to selected deans and appropriate department chairs and to other colleagues in her professional networks. She followed up by telephoning or e-mailing deans and chairs at the top education schools and colleges, asking them to recommend their best graduates for the new positions. Informally, she contacted promising faculty members who might be interested in making a move.

Sonia also identified regional and national professional association meetings likely to draw job seekers and provided funds for search committee chairs to attend. They recruited candidates and held informal screening interviews. She, herself, attended two national conferences to meet informally with potential candidates and to ask colleagues to recommend potential applicants.

When applications began coming in, Sonia made a daily practice of checking the files. When she came across an outstanding applicant, she added the name to her private list of "Potential Hires." If those select candidates failed to appear as finalists, she lobbied search committees to bring them in for interviews. A few search committee members groused privately about the dean's "sticking her nose into our business," but they went ahead and added the dean's recommendations to their "finalist candidates" list. Sonia was still in the "honeymoon" phase of her deanship and faculty members wanted to go along with her choices.

The entire faculty was involved in the interviews. Sonia insisted that each candidate teach a class, give a scholarly presentation to the faculty, and meet with the search committee, department chair, and with her. Faculty members were also invited to socialize with the candidates in informal receptions. Search committee members had dinner with each candidate. Most faculty members placed emphasis on the teaching session and informal get-togethers. They wanted to make sure that both students and faculty liked the applicant. Faculty members were surprised when the dean attended almost every session.

In her private meetings with candidates, Sonia listened as they discussed past experiences and future goals. She pressed hard to determine their commitment to scholarly work and discovered that a few candidates did not have much interest. She began to worry that the search committees might recommend candidates that neither she nor the president would want to hire. She wanted to ensure that she had maximum influence in who was finally selected for the positions.

The first semester raced by in a blur of activity. Candidate pools were larger and better than anyone had anticipated. While faculty were gratified that so many good candidates were interested, they began to wonder out loud whether these "hot shots" would fit in.

When all the candidates were interviewed, Sonia met with the search committees and department chairs and thanked them for their hard work. She explained what would happen from here out. "The next step is for you to recommend three to five finalists to your department chair. I will then ask each chair to submit an unranked list of at least three names. I'd appreciate it if you would share your impressions with me via e-mail over the next week. After hearing from you, and in consultation with the department chair and president, I will make the final decision and negotiate the offer. As soon as I have a firm acceptance, I'll inform you immediately. Again, thanks for all the time, effort, thought, and care you have put into this incredibly demanding process. There is nothing more important that any of us can do to improve our school and university."

Search committee members and department chairs were stunned by Sonia's announcement. Before Sonia came, education faculty members all voted on the candidates and submitted one name to the chair who passed it on to the dean for rubber-stamp action. The president almost always went along with the dean's recommendation. If the top candidate declined the offer, the search committee selected a second choice and, if necessary, repeated the process until they found an acceptable and willing candidate. If no one worked out, a non-tenure track lecturer was hired and a new search began.

John Squire, one of the oldest faculty members and a search committee chair, strongly objected. "Sonia, I don't think you understand. That's not how things are done around here. We're a democratic school. Faculty members determine who is hired, not administrators. You've turned everything upside down."

Taken aback, Sonia responded with obvious emotion, "John, I've put more effort into recruiting and selecting good candidates than anyone in this room. I did so because I believe it is my most important responsibility. When I was hired, the president told me it was my primary responsibility to bring in outstanding new faculty."

John fumed, "Outstanding new faculty members? What are we? Chopped liver? You've undermined our procedures and stepped on toes throughout this entire process. Anyway, why do you think this school needs to change? We thought it was pretty good before you came. You better reconsider your decision. We thought you were a leader, not a dictator."

Sonia could sense the anger rising in the group. She felt strongly she was right, but did not want to continue the argument in such a highly charged atmosphere. "I can see that this discussion is not going anywhere. We're all going to regret it if we continue. However, we do need to get moving on our job offers. Since we seem to be at an impasse, I'll ask the president to clarify the university's hiring procedures for all of us. I'll invite the president to meet with us within the week."

As so often happens in universities, the president was unable to meet with the dean and faculty right away. Two weeks went by before he showed up. During that time, the entire school learned of Sonia's plans to require an unranked short list of candidates and reacted predictably. The faculty unanimously opposed the change and felt that the dean had exceeded her authority. Discussions in the halls, in faculty offices, and meetings in faculty homes expressed anger. Everyone was incensed that the dean would abrogate long-held traditions. Sonia's message that the school "needs to change" by bringing in "outstanding faculty members" had hurt a lot of feelings.

Sonia scheduled the president to meet the faculty the first day after he returned. She also tried to schedule an hour with him prior to the meeting. She was upset when the president's secretary called to say he had a family emergency and could not meet with her. The secretary assured Sonia that the president would attend the faculty meeting.

The president arrived late, as usual, and expressed his apologies. Sonia began the meeting: "I've invited the president here to clarify the university policies on faculty hiring so we're all reading from the same page." She turned the meeting over to him.

The president began, "I was sorry to hear that there are some disagreements about how a search process should proceed. John Squire reached me at home last night and filled me in on the issues. I believe that together we can solve this problem and agree on a process acceptable to everyone.

"Everyone at this university knows I fully support my administrators. Sonia has done a marvelous job of recruiting excellent candidates. I want to thank Sonia and members of the search committees for bringing in a superb applicant pool. All of us share a commitment to making this the best School of Education in the state. And we all know that a strong faculty is essential to make it happen. The issue is not this common goal, but rather the process followed to reach it.

"I'm not going to pontificate. But I do think it is important to remember that excellent universities thrive on full faculty participation. We all have a role to play in making key decisions to ensure that we make sound choices. How should this process work? Every dean in our university has hiring authority. The dean makes the offer and negotiates the contract after consulting with the provost and me. But, every faculty member also has an integral role to play. Search committees are structured to represent faculty interests. They select candidates to interview and determine how the candidates stack up against one another. Search committee members are the experts on the relative merits of candidates. For this reason, the practice in our university is that the search committees decide on the rank ordering of the top candidates in consultation with the appropriate department chair.

"This system works fine most of the time here because deans, department chairs, and search committees almost always agree. Now, however, I realize we need to figure out how to handle situations when there is disagreement. Here's my suggestion. The search committee sends the dean a list of the top three to five candidates and chooses whether to rank them or not. If the committee does rank the candidates and the dean opposes the ranking, the dean meets with the appropriate department chair and search committee to discuss the reasons for the disagreement. After the dean leaves, the search committee members and department chair rank the top three candidates again. The dean then follows the rank order approved by a majority of committee members and endorsed by the department chair. If the number one candidate declines the offer, the dean then contacts the next candidate. If none of the top three candidates accepts the position, the dean can appoint a lecturer and decide whether to conduct a new search the following year.

"This process preserves faculty participation. At the same time, it gives the dean an opportunity to make her case and maintains the right of the dean to negotiate with the candidate and make the final offer. I don't expect anyone to be totally satisfied with this suggested process. It's a happy medium and compromise means that everyone gives as well as gains.

"I want to give you time to think about this suggestion. But our time is limited. We want to nab our first choices before some other university beats us to the punch. Anyone with reactions to the process I've just outlined please let me know by Friday. I'll send you a memo formalizing the final procedure by no later than the middle of next week"

With that, the president left. Others followed, leaving Sonia alone in the room, seething. She felt double-crossed. Sonia recognized that she needed to calm down before deciding what to do next. She returned to her office and called some of her education dean colleagues seeking their advice. All agreed that the president undermined her authority and questioned how she could continue under such conditions. After the calls, Sonia became angrier. She went home and spent the evening writing her letter of resignation.

Later, when the president asked her to meet with him, Sonia politely declined. When he pressed her she said, "I can't work for a president who cuts off my legs in front of the faculty. As I promised in my letter of resignation, I'll continue serving as dean until the end of the academic year, but I'm returning to my old job next August."

STARTING OUT ON THE RIGHT FOOT

A former dean once reflected: "Being a new dean is like learning to ice skate in full view of your faculty" (Wolverton and Gmelch, 2002, p. 25). Everyone expects the new dean to suffer a few bruises. Some leadership gurus argue that it's too soon to have made enemies and mistakes will be forgiven. They recommend taking advantage of this "honeymoon period" to make bold changes right away. But most scholars (and deans) disagree.

Becoming socialized into the dean's role, especially at a new university, requires time and a whole lot of effort. While some new deans will proceed more quickly than others, all go through a period of transition before they are fully assimilated into their new jobs. Although change is rarely easy, it is especially difficult to implement change during this period.

People resist change for good reasons. Change makes people feel incompetent, anxious, and powerless. It generates confusion and conflict. Change also creates a sense of loss (Bolman and Deal, 2003, p. 373). No wonder leaders who initiate change have been described as "masochistic" (Cheldelin, 2000, p. 55). Still, the desire to improve an organization is probably one of the main motives for becoming a leader. Moreover, in this fast-paced world of ours, change is happening at break-neck speed. The salient issue for deans and chairs, like leaders in all organizations, is making sure that the changes that take place in their schools and departments are the right ones. Sonia's experience provides some direction for new deans and chairs.

LEADERSHIP LESSONS

Avoid Making Hasty Decisions

Sonia acted before she was ready. Making hasty decisions is probably the most common mistake new leaders make (Steeples, 1999, p. 19). Sonia had only been on the job a few weeks before she began flexing her muscles and making changes in the hiring process. Like Julie, she looked through only one frame, the structural frame. Sonia relied exclusively on her "position power"—rarely enough to get the job done. In trying to figure out why so many administrators latch onto the structural frame, Berquist explains that, "structural change is organizationally seductive." He warns that although structural change is often easily implemented, employees are not always the "victims;" they can also be "successful saboteurs"—an accurate description of John Squire (Berquist 1992, p 190).

Get to Know the Faculty and Staff and Build Relationships

In assuming a new position, you have to begin by going through the "getting to know you" stage (Wolverton et.al. 2001, p. 98). Learning about the people in your new university and building relationships with them are the number one and two priorities in your first few months on the job. This is the time that you set the tone of your administration. Do you meet faculty members only in your office or do you meet in their offices as well? Do you care about faculty and staff members as human beings? Are you a listener or a talker? Do you take yourself too seriously? Do you have a sense of humor? A positive tone helps build trust and your reputation as a human resources leader. Making others feel important is a tried and true strategy for building trust. Conversely, failing to acknowledge the value of your colleagues before you announce changes is a sure-fire way to fail (Leaming, 1999, pp. 441–43).

Trust is reciprocal. You're not going to get it unless you give it. We should not be surprised to learn that Sonia was not trusted. It is almost painful to recall Sonia's presentations to the faculty. Most of her sentences began with "I." "I know that the most important decisions I make will be our new hires." "I will do everything in my power to ensure that we bring in strong candidates." Let's imagine the subtext faculty heard. "She thinks we don't care about hiring good faculty members." "Sonia thinks we're a third-rate faculty." Or, as John Squire put it, "What are we? Chopped liver?"

Study the Culture and History

Sonia did not appreciate that changing the dean's influence over the hiring process threatened the culture and the very identity of her new college. She was ignorant about the college's history. Sonia didn't even glance through the symbolic window. That was a shame because hearing stories about her "pre-emeritus" predecessor would have helped her understand that the college had functioned for many years in a state of decentralized anarchy. No one had been in charge for a very long time.

Understanding the modus operandi in her new school, Sonia may have sought different changes. For example, she may have asked the president to delay faculty searches. That would have given her time to learn more about the unit's culture and build trust with faculty members. Or, perhaps she would have exercised her political skills and bargained with the search committees to extend her influence over selection decisions. However, it is pretty difficult to be a successful political leader when you are distrusted by your colleagues and ignorant about your organization's culture and history.

Ask the Boss for Help and for Clear Expectations

We realize that there are always two sides to any story. As Tucker and Bryan (1988) quip, "most academic stories actually have eleven sides" (p. 92). Sonia may not look pretty in this scenario, but the president looks downright ugly. Where was the president when Sonia met with the faculty the first time? Why didn't he introduce Sonia to them? Why didn't he tell them how elated he was that she had accepted the position and what he charged her to do? Why didn't he share information about the college's culture with Sonia and introduce her to key people on campus that would help her learn more?

Unfortunately, deans often live with half-hearted support from the "higher-ups. The good news to aspiring deans, however, is that in the first few months on the job, the president and provost are often as anxious to impress you as you are to impress them. This is the time when a new dean can ask for help. If the president or provost does not volunteer to introduce you to your faculty and other key people or give you information about the culture, it is up to you to ask them to do so. Ask your boss to explain his or her expectations for your first couple of years on the job. If you have concerns, voice them.

Keep the Higher-Ups Informed Orally and in Writing

Don't follow Sonia's example. Tell your provost and president what you need to implement the changes they (and hopefully, you) want. Keep them informed of your progress and make sure you have their full support at every stage of the change process. When they assign a task, especially one that requires you to implement a major change, write a memo explaining the steps you plan to take to accomplish it and invite their suggestions and concerns. Make these plans as specific as possible. Your memo can serve as an informal contract. It may not prevent you from being double-crossed, but it will make your boss think twice before doing so.

SUMMING UP

Looking through multiple frames we saw: a new dean wedded to the structural frame, convinced that her "position power" and promised presidential support were sufficient to "call the shots"; a university president so afraid to navigate in political waters that he double-crossed his new dean rather than deal with conflict; an angry and hurt faculty convinced that their new dean was a human relations' disaster; and no one attending to the important symbolic task of sharing the history and culture. Both Sonia and the president paid a steep price for this bungled change effort. Sonia's career was derailed—at least temporarily and her confidence took a blow. The president lost a promising new dean.

Although we would like to believe that Sonia's story is unique, we have seen it played out time and time again. New deans have been called "amateurs" because typically they have no formal preparation for their position and rarely any experience in a dean's office. Their socialization is "random" and "capricious." Too often, new deans learn the ropes in isolation. Some higher education scholars have recommended that universities provide part-time apprenticeships for dean interns, overlap terms to allow the retiring dean to mentor the new dean, and promote opportunities for deans to meet with one another (Wolverton et.al. 2001, p. 100). We support all these ideas, but our favorite is that new deans study how very successful, experienced deans operate. It is for this reason that we turn now from a new dean to an experienced dean who knows his job very well. He's been in it for over twenty years. Let's see how he relies on all the frames to successfully implement a significant instructional change.

STUDIO CLASSROOMS FOR A COLLEGE OF SCIENCE AND MATHEMATICS

When Phil stepped into the new chemistry studio classroom, his face lit up. Small groups of students buzzed with activity. With thirty-two new computers, the professor's instructions for the day and course materials were easily accessible. Electrical connections to lab equipment, helium gas lines, and de-ionized water ran to the six octagonal clusters.

Even though Phil was dean of the College of Science and Mathematics, the young professor barely looked up when Phil walked in. Matt was too busy working with students. He referred one group to the class home page where course materials were stored. Matt reminded another group to check his instructions for the day's lesson on their posted schedule. Phil was pleased to see that Matt's time was spent helping individual students and small groups as they grappled with the problems he had assigned earlier in the week.

What a refreshing change from the traditional lecture/laboratory approach common in most science classrooms, Phil thought. For a moment, a vision of the "old" classroom clouded his memory. Gone were rows upon rows of benches where students madly scribbled notes as the professor talked, then worked in isolation in a lab. Now, students were talking—to one another and to their instructor. It certainly was noisier, but Phil preferred it that way. Everyone was engaged helping one another and able to get the professor's attention when needed.

How did this sea change happen? Who made it happen? Why didn't the "nay-sayers" sabotage the project? Phil credits the university president for sparking a "sense of urgency" to reform teaching and learning in the College of Science and Mathematics. As the top administrator of a polytechnic university, the president was certain that a strong background in science and mathematics was an essential foundation for twenty-first century jobs. He shared the dean's determination to make their university a leader of technologically current and student-centered learning.

Studio classrooms were the right idea at the right time. They encompassed new information technology and current trends in pedagogical reform of higher education. Its roots went back more than a decade. A few faculty members in the college (mainly older, tenured, full professors) started an informal study group to examine strategies for improving the quality of instruction. The more they read, the more committed they became to transforming teacher-led classrooms to student-centered classrooms. They learned that studio classrooms, equipped with the latest information technology, could promote student interaction.

The group discovered that Renssalaer Polytechnic Institute (RPI) had just begun to pilot a version of studio classrooms. Phil paid a visit to RPI accompanied by a carefully selected group of his reform-minded faculty members. Some were relatively new; others had been at the institution for more than twenty years. A few had worked on the original study group. All were well respected by colleagues.

Phil and his entourage toured the facilities, talked to students, met with faculty members and administrators. They looked at all aspects of the program. They saw that the architecture, technology, and even the furniture encouraged students to work together. Professors stepped out of the role of lecturer and into the role of facilitator. The visitors left RPI committed to design their own version of studio classrooms.

Shortly thereafter, Phil flew with a group of faculty members to Washington D.C. to explore funding sources. Some travelers were the same people who had visited RPI, but others were new. In D.C. the group met with staff members from major foundations (e.g., the National Science Foundation and the National Institutes of Health) to discuss potential grant support. The group was delighted to learn that their ideas for improving instruction were well received by potential benefactors.

Back on campus, the travelers met and agreed to propose to the faculty that the college initiate studio classrooms. Despite the unanimous enthusiasm of the small band of reformers, Phil was nervous about how to approach the rest of the faculty. His twenty-plus years as dean convinced him that this was not the time to formally ask for faculty approval to design studio classrooms. As Phil put it, "If a change is voted on, most of the time the majority of faculty members will vote against it."

Early in the academic year, Phil and the "cheerleaders" planned a faculty meeting agenda devoted solely to studio classrooms. Four different faculty travelers gave brief reports about what they learned at RPI and in Washington D.C. They presented their impressions of studio classrooms at RPI.

One presenter said, "I know I speak for all of us who visited RPI and had the chance to see students at work in studio classrooms. The students were totally engaged." Another said, "I was impressed with the freedom it gave the professor to meet with each group, checking the students' understanding, and helping them when they got stuck." A senior faculty member from the informal study group chimed in saying, "The findings we have reviewed from a number of studies confirm that more learning takes place in studio classrooms."

Phil agreed with the results. "Students become more interested when they work together and use technology to examine a broad range of information. I think that studio classrooms also are more interesting and enjoyable for faculty. The professor becomes a resource and a facilitator instead of the sole expert with all the answers."

Here, Phil stepped back, smiled, and confessed that he did not expect everyone on the faculty to "jump on the studio-classroom bandwagon." "After all," he admitted, "we may be dead wrong. We won't know until we experiment with our own studio classrooms." He concluded the meeting with a proclamation and an assurance: "Universities should be safe places to experiment. That's what academic freedom's all about. If our experiment with studio classrooms doesn't work, we'll drop it and go back to the drawing board."

Phil kept the president well informed about the progress of the effort. In turn, the president communicated with the chancellor of the state system about the plans for studio classrooms. By the time a small group of faculty members in the college agreed to design studio classrooms, both the president and the chancellor were on board. The president allocated $450,000 and the chancellor came up with $250,000. Faculty members wrote successful grant proposals to bring the total up to over a million dollars for remodeling and equipping the studio classrooms.

Phil encouraged faculty members to volunteer for the arduous tasks of designing the curriculum and instructing the first classes. In chemistry, Matt, a young, untenured faculty member, agreed to design and teach the chemistry class if Phil could answer three questions to his satisfaction: (1) What effect will participation in this change have on my retention and eventual tenure and promotion? (2) How can I find time to launch this new program? (3) Will I have enough resources to give the studio-classroom approach a chance to succeed?

In response, Phil gave, in his words, "the shirt off my back." He assured Matt full support from the dean, provost, and president for retention. Assuming Matt did a credible job in the studio classroom and his other assignments, Phil told Matt he could expect approval when he applied for tenure and promotion. But guaranteeing support for retention, tenure, and promotion (RTP) is easier said than done. "Counting" work in studio classrooms required a revision of the RTP criteria. Phil made the revision himself and once again avoided a meeting for faculty members to discuss and vote on the revision. Instead, Phil sent copies of the revised RTP criteria to all tenured full and associate professors in the unit. He asked them to review the additional criterion: "contributing to the reform of instruction through participation in studio classrooms." Phil asked faculty members to put questions or disagreements in writing and send them to him within six weeks. Receiving none, he forwarded the revised RTP criteria to the provost for approval. The provost was happy to approve it.

Phil provided other ongoing support for the instructors in studio classrooms. He lightened their teaching loads to give them time to plan the curriculum. He allocated a small operating expense budget for equipment and student assistants.

Looking back on his efforts to support the college's first chemistry studio classroom, Phil surmised that "protecting" studio classroom instructors from negative faculty members by revising the RTP criteria was paramount. Next in importance was protecting the "naysayers" from pressure to abandon their traditional methods. He admonished the "cheerleaders" to "tone down" their criticism of skeptical faculty. He reminded them that most of the negative reaction was coming from older faculty members who were solid traditional teachers and hard workers. Phil warned, "You won't help your cause by belittling your colleagues."

In a faculty meeting, one of the innovative supporters announced that the traditional lecture/lab approach was "bankrupt." Phil publicly disagreed. "All of us are the products of the lecture/lab system," he said, "and higher education in the U.S. is respected around the world. We must have been doing something right. Of course, there's always room for improvement. Studio classrooms are one avenue for enhancing instruction, but just like the lecture/laboratory method, it is not the only way."

Phil believed most of the resisters could be won over—in time. He left hardcore opponents alone. He invited borderline professors into the studio classrooms and encouraged them to stick around long enough to make an informed judgment. Phil spent time in the hallways and in faculty members' offices explaining the rationale for the change and listening to concerns and suggestions.

Phil allocated travel funds to pay for reformers' expenses when they presented papers about their "experiment" to professional associations. He even co-presented with faculty members at a couple of national conferences. Phil distributed publications related to the college's new studio classrooms to all the college's faculty members, the university president, chancellor, and colleague deans in science and mathematics at other institutions. Before long, visitors began coming to observe the studio classrooms in action. The university president brought alumni, potential donors, CEO's from around the state, and his own external cabinet members to see the change first-hand. He was proud of helping the university become a model for innovative instruction in math and the sciences.

After the first year's success in chemistry and math, members of the physics and statistics departments began working on designing studio classrooms for their majors. Phil hosted a ceremony to launch the new studio classrooms and to celebrate the excellent results from the first year. Everyone in the College of Science and Mathematics received an invitation. Since the food was great, the program brief, and the president in attendance, faculty turn out was well above average.

Phil started the program with testimonials from students. They enthusiastically praised their instructors and the entire college for designing studio classrooms. Involved faculty members presented charts showing greater learning gains in studio vs. traditional classes in the same subject areas. The president offered his blessings: "Congratulations are in order. The undergraduate education our students receive in the College of Science and Mathematics is one of the best in the United States. Your studio classrooms are becoming a magnet for your colleagues in other institutions. You should be proud of yourselves. I certainly am very proud of you."

Later, Phil noticed that instruction in the "traditional" classes was beginning to change, too. Although lectures and labs remained central, many professors fostered more student interaction, introduced collaborative work groups, and expanded the technology used in their classes.

DISSECTING THE SUCCESS STORY

We often hear that "change is inevitable." Perhaps some changes are. But the changes described in this scenario were not. Anyone who has tried to introduce an instructional innovation in a university knows that it is never easy. How did Phil succeed? Let's take a look through our four frames, beginning with the political frame.

Phil was a consummate politician. By recasting change as an experiment, Phil defused the opposition. He believed that the majority of the faculty would vote against studio classrooms and they would never see the light of day. Instead of following the official college approval structure, Phil circumvented it. He and his band of reformers presented their plans as an information item to the faculty. Similarly, when Phil wanted to add work in studio classrooms to the criteria for promotion and tenure, no vote was taken. Phil simply sent the faculty his proposed addition and gave them the chance to respond to it in writing.

Phil did not want faculty members to make a decision about studio class-rooms in a meeting because past experiences convinced him that negativism flourishes in large groups. He saw naysayers dominate too often. Phil under-stood why faculty members are reluctant to speak in favor of an innovation. Some believe that the negative faculty members know more than they do and do not want to risk being put down in a meeting. Untenured faculty members are reluctant to publicly oppose senior faculty members for fear they won't be recommended for promotion or tenure. Most faculty members believe that it is not their job to deal with conflict. That's what administrators get paid for.

Our message is not that deans can or should avoid meetings. In universi-ties, meetings are the most common arena for internal politics and faculty members want and expect to be heard. Politically astute deans, however, will make sure that they have a clear agenda and influential supporters for their position before an issue is debated. If the dean is voted down too many times, that dean is not going to last.

By calling the "change" an "experiment," Phil avoided dividing his col-lege into "winners" and "losers." The experimenters could "do their thing" without casting those not involved as "losers." Besides, what self-respecting academician can oppose experimentation? Well, as Phil suspected, some did. But, he stood up for the critics of the studio-classroom "experiment." In doing so, he acknowledged the value of the traditional culture—quite a contrast to Sonia's behavior.

Phil showed a sophisticated understanding of the human relations frame by supporting the entire faculty, advocates for studio classrooms as well as skeptics. He asked the "cheer leaders" to tone down their criticism of their colleagues and, at the same time, commended studio-classroom instructors. Whenever Phil spoke about studio classrooms, he made participating faculty members feel important. Making others feel important is not difficult to do and it is a terrific motivator (Leaming, 2002, p. 443). For the innovators, Phil gave support that truly makes a difference to faculty members: time to implement an innovation, resources to sustain it, and points for promotion and tenure.

Phil understood how to use the vertical structure to support studio class-rooms. Getting the president and the chancellor involved from the beginning was more than just good luck. Phil capitalized on their interest to communicate a sense of urgency and expand financial resources for studio classrooms. Phil also demonstrated his understanding of the structural frame by aligning the retention, tenure. and promotion criteria to encourage untenured faculty mem-bers to teach in studio classrooms. Phil was also the quintessential symbolic leader. He conveyed his passion for studio classrooms in the stories he told, the faculty members and students he recognized, and the ceremonies he hosted.

LEADERSHIP LESSONS

Today, there are many people who deserve credit for launching this successful innovation. But Phil was the key person. He shaped his campaign for studio classrooms by blending strategies from all four of the frames with confidence, enthusiasm, and insight. All of us who want to promote change can learn some valuable lessons from Phil. In conclusion, we share our list knowing there are other lessons just as valuable.

It's OK to Start Small

Don't wait to win over everybody or even the majority in your unit before you initiate a change. Work with those willing to work with you. In many cases that means working with people whom you believe need changing the least (Farson, 1996, p. 88). That's fine because they are more likely to be successful and, ultimately, will help win over their reluctant colleagues.

Bring the Higher-ups on Board ASAP

Get the "ducks in line," especially the "head ducks" before you launch the change effort. Invite the president and provost to speak to the faculty to help you garner support. Keep them informed at every stage of the change process.

Minimize Meetings

Unless you know that the majority of your faculty is in favor of the change, avoid giving the opponents a public forum to vent. Instead of relying on meetings to give faculty members a chance to express their views, ask for written responses. You will hear from fewer faculty members. Those who take the time to respond will be more thoughtful. Don't worry too much about faculty resistance. Most faculty members are delighted when a meeting is cancelled.

Protect the "Naysayers"

Everyone expects you to support the "cheerleaders." They don't expect you to protect the critics. Change efforts usually divide the faculty into "insiders and outsiders" and "winners and losers." When you support faculty members who do not support you, you defuse the opposition. You also may win some of them over.

Practice "Big You, Little Me"

Giving credit to others is almost always a good thing for a dean to do, but is especially important when trying to implement change. Host ceremonies to celebrate short-term wins and recognize the 'movers and shakers.' Making others feel important is a way to make certain the change you support will become important to others.

Chapter 4

Faculty

Confronting Creeps and Cliques

SCENES FROM THE LIFE OF A BELEAGUERED CHAIR

Kurt Russell is a tenured, senior faculty member at a small, Midwest public university. He was recently a favored candidate for the Marketing Department chair position in the College of Business. To his surprise, he lost the election to Peter, a relatively new, untenured professor. His defeat to an inexperienced colleague hit him hard. Kurt has still not recovered from this stinging blow to his pride and ambition.

At a recent faculty meeting, Peter asked for ideas to improve the department's fund-raising campaign. Kurt smirked as he retorted, "C'mon Peter, wise up. We're not going to get any money. If any funds are raised, the dean will decide where they go. And, in case you haven't noticed, the dean doesn't like us. This is a complete waste of time. The only reason you're trying to involve us in fund raising is because you were told to. We need to spend our time doing what we were hired to do: teach and research."

Peter reacted quickly: "Kurt, I don't share your pessimism. It's important to our students and faculty to get more financial support. By the way, I neglected to mention that 10 percent of all funds raised goes to faculty members for their own professional development. This includes travel money. You've been trying to get support for attending our national conference. This is your chance." Kurt laughed and said, "Good try, Peter but I'm not holding my breath."

This was not Kurt's only challenge to Peter's authority. At an earlier faculty meeting Peter announced his choice for speaker at the annual departmental symposium. Kurt challenged Peter's decision. "Everyone knows that speaker is boring and out of date. Boy, you can sure pick a loser. Peter," Kurt sneered. "There must be dozens of speakers who would be better for our symposium. Don't look now, but your inexperience is showing again." Peter looked anxiously at the faculty hoping that someone would say something positive about the speaker and support his decision. No one said a word. "Well, Kurt, I'm really in a predicament here. I've already issued the invitation and the speaker has accepted. I'm sorry you feel so negative, but it's too late to back out now."

Kurt's negativity was not confined to meetings. He used every opportunity to cross swords with the chair. When Peter distributed the first draft of a new internship program, he asked faculty members to provide their reactions to the proposal. Kurt responded first, sending his e-mail to the chair, and, in addition, to all department members and the dean. Kurt predicted that the program would be a "disaster." Specifically, he claimed that there was insufficient attention given to the selection process and to the supervision of students during their internship.

Peter immediately e-mailed Kurt and sent copies to all the recipients of Kurt's negative note. He thanked Kurt for his response and reported that the president of the local Chamber of Commerce brought up some of the same problems. He asked Kurt to chair a task force to redesign the program. In Kurt's reply, he refused the job and accused Peter of trying to co-opt him.

Peter was disappointed that Kurt's colleagues did not attempt to censure or confront his behavior. He knew that Kurt had supporters among older faculty and was aware that the vote for the chair's position had been close. Kurt had been at the university ten years longer. He was knowledgeable about how the university worked and was friendly with upper-level administrators. Every day he had lunch with a group of the "good old boys" in the department.

Kurt reveled in playing the political game. Once he knew Peter's position on almost any issue, he quickly and loudly voiced his opposition. He spent a lot of time cultivating faculty support. Peter was aware of this because some faculty members reported Kurt's attempts to win them over and turn them against the chair. They told Peter that Kurt started rumors to put Peter in a bad light. The latest rumor was that Peter was bringing on a new administrative assistant and expanding office space for his staff. Fanning the flames, the "faculty informers" accused Peter of "empire building" and warned that some faculty members would end up sharing office space.

Peter found Kurt's contentiousness and relentless criticism wearing. He began to doubt his ability to chair the department. Despite repeated attempts to win Kurt over, ignore him, or deflect his attacks, Kurt's behavior did not change. Peter kept hoping that at least one faculty member would confront

Kurt, but no one did. The faculty reaction reminded him of a sad commentary he had read recently written by a former dean: "Already as a faculty member and before my administrative stint, I had been dismayed by the cowardice among my colleagues" (Martin, 1988, p. 39).

Peter realizes that his negativity and depression are affecting other faculty members. Fewer and fewer faculty members attend department meetings. At times, the department does not even have a quorum and must delay critical decisions needing immediate action. The energy and excitement immediately following his election have disappeared. Not as many faculty members drop in to see him. When Peter walks around to talk informally with faculty members, he notices that there is less joking and chatting in the halls. His department is becoming a gloomy place to work. Peter is stumped. He doesn't know why Kurt is so difficult, and he is running out of ideas about how to deal with him. His health is beginning to suffer; he is losing both sleep and his sense of humor. Peter's wife is getting tired of spending every night listening to him stew. Peter is seriously considering resigning his position.

THE PETER-KURT TUSSLE IN PERSPECTIVE

The severity of problems generated by a few faculty members is a well-known fact in most colleges and universities. Page Smith's incisive critique, *Killing the Spirit: Higher Education in America,* cuts to the nub: "We often talk of the 'academic community,' whereas there is no community but only atomized individuals known as specialists who hardly talk to each other, let alone to their colleagues in other fields." He quotes Irving Babbit who portrays members of a "modern college faculty as a collection of 'infinitely repellant particles'" (Smith, 1990, p. 16).

Set in this context, Kurt's behavior toward Peter is not unusual. Nor is Peter's reaction. But most academic leaders are at a loss of how to deal with their "Kurts" without allowing them to sap their energy and self-confidence as well as poison the morale of an entire department.

Typically, chairs and deans define negative faculty behavior as a human relations problem: "We have a personality conflict," they say. While that may be true, it is usually only the tip of the iceberg. Other frames suggest alternative explanations. Using a multi-frame analysis also offers different ways of handling the problem.

When we were kids on the playground and saw someone picking on someone else the way that Kurt picked on Peter, we all would have known immediately who Kurt was. In those long-gone, but not always idyllic days, we would have called Kurt a "bully."

In her practical book, *The College Administrator's Survival Guide* (2006), Gunsalus defines bullies as "people who are willing to cross the boundaries of civilized behavior that inhibit others" (p. 122). She compares bullying behavior to other serious personnel problems, for example, chemical dependency or domestic abuse. Sadly, universities have more than their fair share of bullies. Gunsalus (2006) identifies the decentralized structure of universities as one factor in the breeding ground for faculty bullies. A second support is the prominence given to the concepts of "academic freedom" and "collegiality" and the inherent opportunities afforded petty tyrants to manipulate them (p. 124).

The most common reaction to bullies and the turbulence they spawn in academe is avoidance. The political frame offers some insight into why avoidance is such a popular reaction. Bullies provoke confrontation. Peter is not the only department chair frightened of conflict and reluctant to confront discord head-on. But we know from studying the political frame that conflict in any human organization is inevitable (Bolman and Deal, 2003, p. 15). Instead of trying to eradicate discord, Higgerson (1996) recommends that chairs and deans learn how to manage conflict, channeling energy through confrontation, bargaining, and compromise (pp. 140–41).

Kurt is obviously savvy politically and knows how to build coalitions and support for his negative agenda. Peter, on the other hand, seems unable to rally people to his positions. He is engaged in a battle with Kurt for control of the department, but he fails to develop a strategy for consolidating his power. Peter should have called Kurt on his bullying behavior and confronted him with consequences for his actions. Gunsalus (2006) maintains that most bullies are rarely confronted on their behavior or told what will happen if it continues. She recommends that administrators outline the points they want to make before meeting with a bully and follow up their meeting with a written memo to the bully, confirming their points (pp. 127–30). A longer-term strategy is prevention. In order to prevent, or at least reduce bullying behavior, a political frame strategy is appropriate: cultivating allies to help create and maintain an environment in which civility is expected and reinforced.

In his irreverent and provocative book about the workplace, Robert Sutton (2007) identifies bullies as an "especially nasty species." Their impact on organizations is so devastating because "they sap people of their energy and esteem" (p. 29). Studies in the corporate world found that bullies cost companies dearly. Their legacy is the loss of creativity, innovation, cooperation, and motivation (Sutton, 2007, pp. 49–50). The destructive, cumulative effects derive from two factors: one, nasty interactions make a far greater impression on us ("five times the punch") than positive interactions

(Sutton, 2007, p. 30); and two, these undesirable characters "breed like rabbits" (Sutton, 2007, p. 66).

He notes that many top corporations have written policies to ensure "a jerk-free workplace." A rule can be simple: for example, "Everyone in this company will be treated with respect;" "Employees should respect and support each other even if they don't like each other" (Sutton, 2007, p. 59). These values can be woven structurally into hiring and retention policies. The companies that not only post their "rule," but also follow up by responding immediately if any individual degrades another, have had considerable success in cleaning out bullies (Sutton, 2007, pp. 59–60). Universities might do well to emulate these efforts to hammer out and enforce guidelines for professional interaction. Certainly, Peter would have been wise to do so.

Leadership Lessons

What can chairs and deans learn from Peter's struggle? Just as the frames helped us gain a fuller understanding of the Peter/Kurt tussle, looking through the different lenses also generates more options.

Recognize your Authority

Peter behaved as if he subscribed to the "pernicious myth" that chairs are powerless. They are not, but their effectiveness is drastically reduced if they think they are (Lucas, 1994, p. 18). The structural frame reminds us that chairs have authority over many areas dear to a professor's heart, including assignment of classes, the class schedule, the department's operating expenses, office space, and faculty evaluation. For example, although Kurt is already a tenured, full professor, Peter will assess his performance for post-tenure review and possibly make recommendations for merit pay—assuming Peter lasts that long as chair.

Share Problems with your Supervisor and Colleagues

Taking a closer look through the structural lens, we can visualize some positive scenes. In the university structure, a department chair reports to the dean and works closely with other department chairs. Peter acted in isolation, but a supervisor needs to know about serious personnel problems. Had Peter kept his dean informed about his problem with Kurt, the dean probably would have supported Peter and may have helped him. With the support of his boss, we suspect that Peter would have been courageous enough to confront Kurt. Other department chairs also could have assisted our struggling chair. By discussing the "Kurt problem" with a few other chairs, Peter could have checked his perceptions about the situation and sought advice from more experienced and trusted colleagues.

Surface the Attack

The human resources perspective recommends communicating openly and testing assumptions. The political frame advises learning how to manage conflict. A couple of strategies in line with these recommendations are to "surface the attack" and to "seek group confirmation or denial." Either is preferable to avoidance (Branson 1981, p. 30). For example, how would Kurt have reacted in the meeting about fund-raising if Peter had asked him, "Kurt, your statement accusing me of being naïve sounded insulting. Did you mean to insult me?" Surfacing Kurt's attack with a question would have given Kurt the chance to back down. Most of the time bullies deny that they intended to attack or insult. If Kurt refused to back down, he would have been forced to admit he was being insulting. Who wants to admit that?

Seek Confirmation or Denial from Group

Another effective strategy for managing conflict is to seek confirmation or denial from the group of the bully's opinions. For example, Peter could have asked faculty members if they agreed with Kurt's negative assessment of the symposium speaker. If no one indicated that they agreed with Kurt, Peter might have said, "Looks like you're a minority of one, Kurt. You don't have to attend, but it seems like your colleagues want the opportunity to hear him." However, if many others supported Kurt's position, then Peter might have to reconsider his invitation to hear the speaker or agree to invite someone less controversial into the next symposium.

Learn about the Unit's History and Culture

Evidently, symbolic issues were outside Peter's zone of awareness. Like Sonia, Peter should have realized that he was chair of a department whose culture was formed well before his time. A quick study of the department's history, talking to people about the recent and distant past, would have helped him ferret out elusive core values and identify important heroes or heroines, past or present, that are looked to for a sense of direction and continuity.

Accentuate the Positive

Once culturally aware, Peter could have told stories illustrating the Marketing Department's core values, and, at the same time, spread good news about the department. He could have blunted some of Kurt's sting by targeting multiple, audiences making his own faculty the primary source and recipient of the favorable publicity. Stories can boost morale, especially stories that make people feel important and valued. When faculty members learn more about positive things happening in their department, they become less tolerant of a consistently negative colleague.

Use Rituals to Manage Conflict

Ritual is another source of cultural leverage that Peter might look to. Rituals create order, clarity, and predictability and create bonds even among people that don't get along (Bolman and Deal, 2003, p. 406). One ritual Peter might consider is to start each faculty meeting with a five to ten minute period for "appreciation and grievances." This ritualistic beginning allows anyone to express gratitude to a colleague for a particularly commendable or helpful action. A time to bring up grievances follows expressions of appreciation. In the grievance period, participants are given a chance to get things that have been bothering them "off their chests." Had Peter instituted this ritual, he could have responded to Kurt's angry criticisms by asking him to save "those kinds of comments" for the next "appreciation and grievances" period. This ritual has the advantage of minimizing interruptions and allowing work to proceed without stifling free speech.

The symbolic frame views meetings as "sacred occasions to celebrate and transform the culture." Peter needed to work on building a sense of community in his department. But a "community" depends upon members knowing, trusting, and respecting one another. Unfortunately, faculty members in the same department frequently do not get to know one another except on the most superficial level. Peter might have considered adopting the "featured faculty" ritual. It helps faculty members learn more about one another and does not have to take much time. Five minutes is reserved in departmental meetings to allow one faculty member to share anything about him or her self. Over time, the "featured faculty" presentations provide connections and common areas of interest on which to build a collegial culture.

Summing Up

The undeclared war between Peter and Kurt is a classic case of what can happen when two people scrutinize a problem through entirely different lenses. Kurt viewed the department politically. He wanted to wrest power from Peter, or at least guarantee that Peter was unable to exercise power. Peter thought that he and Kurt were having a "personality conflict." His narrow view of the human resources frame deprived him of a clear understanding of the bully problem and the many strategies available to leaders who are multi-frame thinkers. The following case of Diane shows how the ability to operate simultaneously in all four frames advances a leader's chances for success in working with the faculty.

A CHAIR SUCCESSFULLY CONFRONTS DIVISIVENESS

Diane felt overwhelmed by the divisiveness in her department. After one year as chair of the Political Science Department in a large College of Liberal Arts, Diane saw two warring gangs. One, she nicknamed the "old guard." The other, she called the "grant getters."

The majority of the grant getters were younger faculty members. About half had been awarded tenure and the other half were in tenure-track positions. The old guard included mainly senior faculty members, long tenured, with full professor status. Neither group had much affection or respect for members of the other camp.

The old guard resented the grant getters for the recognition the president and dean gave to them. They complained that the grant getters did less and less teaching and failed to shoulder a fair share of departmental work. Most galling to the old guard were the few grant getters who taught only one or two classes a semester. In contrast to the grant getters, the old guard had minimal funds for travel, equipment, or materials. They were demoralized and resentful.

The grant getters argued that they had put the Political Science Department on the map. As a result of their projects, publications, and research assistant positions, better students and better faculty members had been drawn to the department. They offered to compare workloads with the old guard, convinced that their year-round responsibilities for projects would reveal that they put in more hours. The grant getters felt under-appreciated by their old guard colleagues.

A particularly nasty altercation occurred at a department meeting early in the year. Faculty members were discussing criteria for merit pay, and the grant getters were pushing for more emphasis on publications. A member of the old guard took the stage and exclaimed that he thought the author, Flannery O'Connor, right on target when she said, "Everywhere I go I'm asked if I think that universities stifle writers. My opinion is that they don't stifle enough of them."

A grant getter responded. "I'm astonished that you used a quotation from a book. I knew that you had never written anything, at least anything that has been published, and for years I've suspected that you have never read anything either. Did you dig out that quotation out of a book you read when you were an undergrad?"

Diane was painfully aware that the reputation of the political science department was slipping. Stories of their conflicts provoked smug laughter from colleagues in other departments. She knew that if the backbiting continued, her dean, the provost, and president would find it difficult to support the department. Whatever the issue, faculty members seemed unable to reach consensus or even discuss issues civilly. Meetings had degenerated into hostility and inertia. Diane decided that it was time to confront the divisiveness and knew she could not do so alone.

Diane called the department's Executive Committee into session. She opened the meeting by saying, "Today, we have a one-item agenda: divisiveness in our department. I have grown more and more alarmed about this. We're unable to reach consensus on just about anything. Instead of working together, we're working against one another. We're becoming a campus joke. I am not amused and I don't think that you are either. I know that you and I can't solve the problem alone, but we can describe its impact, examine its causes, and challenge the faculty to try and resolve it."

Over the next two months, Diane and the committee hammered out a report they called, with some flourish, *Divided We Fall*. In it they chronicled the missed opportunities to hire new faculty members, declining quality of instructional programs, and damage to the department's reputation on the university campus. Committee members targeted the lack of departmental priorities as an underlying cause of the antipathy between the old guard and the grant getters.

Diane called a special meeting of the faculty to present the report. She began, "We're plagued by divisiveness. I'm preoccupied with this problem. All of you are frustrated and frankly, our accomplishments the past couple of years have been minimal. I asked the Executive Committee to help us figure out how to address this problem. They've worked long and hard on the report you have in front of you today: *Divided We Fall*. At this point, I am turning the meeting over to members of the Executive Committee who will present highlights of the report."

Each member of the committee covered different sections of the report, outlining the impact of the problem on students, faculty members, staff members, and the department as a whole. They explained how the lack of agreement on department priorities fuels the divide. The Executive Committee concluded their report by recommending that the entire faculty come together for a full-day work session to reach agreement on top departmental priorities that they could all support.

Following the report's recommendations, Diane scheduled a work-session on a Friday, only two weeks away. She asked each faculty member to review the report before the work session and warned that unless everyone attended, they would not make much progress. While there was some grumbling, every faculty member agreed up to attend. They all recognized that the department's divisiveness was a serious problem. They also wanted to have a voice in setting priorities. Diane scheduled the work session off campus and asked faculty members to leave their cell phones and laptops in the office.

The meeting started promptly at 8:00 a.m. To the surprise of the old guard, the entire faculty quickly agreed that "quality of instruction" was the number one priority of the department. When an old guard faculty member complained that the grant getters did not act as if teaching was a priority, one of the young grant getters responded, "I'd like to do more teaching, but I'm bogged town with the 'administrivia' required by my funding agency. If I could get some assistance running the day-to-day operation of my project, I'd gladly teach more classes."

Seeing the nodding heads agreeing with the young faculty spokesman, Diane made a proposal. "Instead of paying part-time faculty members to teach so many classes, we could allocate the funds we get from grants to pay for administrative assistants and clerical support to help faculty members working on projects." Diane admitted that, "It might take some time to negotiate budget changes with funding agencies to fully implement this plan, but I believe that together we can do this."

Building on the momentum Diane said, "Now that we have made real progress on setting our number one priority, let's see if we can reach agreement on what the minimum teaching load in our department should be." Trusting that Diane would follow through, the grant-getters joined their old guard colleagues to support a minimum teaching load of at least half time.

Diane was elated. She knew that departmental divisiveness would surface around other issues. Nonetheless, simply to have a day when faculty members in both camps actually listened to one another was a milestone. At the end of the work session, Diane announced that the faculty had accomplished a "minor miracle" by having reached consensus so quickly on the department's top priority and its implication for teaching loads.

Diane was true to her word. She recruited and hired administrative assistants and clerical staff to help the grant getters. She publicized her department's number one priority, "quality of instruction," in all departmental, college, and university publications. The president, provost, and dean bragged to alumni and prospective students about the political science department's commitment to teaching. When the time came for budget allocations for the following year, Diane discovered that the political science department received an additional allocation for clerical support and administrative assistants. All in all, she decided, the year ended a lot better than it started.

On the last day of the academic year, Diane hosted a party. Gag gifts were given to each faculty member receiving tenure and or promotion, along with framed certificates. Faculty members "roasted" the one retiree, telling old, but not-forgotten, funny stories. Everyone seemed to have a good time and the party did not break up until the wee hours.

EXAMINING THE MOVE FROM
CONFRONTATION TO CONSENSUS

In *Gone for Good—Tales of University Life After the Golden Age* (1999), Stuart Rojstaczer laments, "We are not, as a group, very capable of interacting with other people, nor are we hired for our ability to work as a team" (p. 159). Every chair and dean we know would say, "Amen" to that. It is much more common to have faculty cliques fighting one another than a united team pulling together. What was Diane's secret? Fortunately, there is no secret. Diane's strategies reflect a judicious blend of actions based upon her understanding of all four frames. Analyzing Diane's strategies provides leadership lessons appropriate to both deans and chairs.

Leadership Lessons

Confront the Problem; Build Support and Provide Incentives for your Agenda

Diane assumed political leadership by having the courage to confront the issue head on. She set the agenda. Devoting several meetings of the Executive Committee to examining the causes and impact of the department's schism, she built a support network. When it came time to bargain and negotiate, Diane was up to speed. The grant getters signed on to the minimum teaching requirement because Diane proposed allocating scarce resources to give them administrative assistant and clerical support. Her negotiating skills helped create a sense of "positive politics."

Don't take Sides and Encourage Ownership of the Problem

Diane relied also on both the structural and the human resources frame. As a human resources leader, she was careful not to take sides. Instead, she emphasized the common goal of healing the department's rift. She capitalized on the faculty's belief that they should participate fully in decision-making in the university's decentralized structure. Diane's "collaborative" approach encouraged faculty members to stop attacking one another and attack the problem instead. Once faculty members faced the consequences of their schism, the common goal of "quality of instruction" emerged quickly. Divisiveness is a symptom of the lack of community, but it is also a cause. Because of Diane and the Executive Committee's insistence that the faculty "own" the problems they had created and work together to solve them, they helped build a sense of community within the department.

Attend to Appearances and Celebrate Accomplishments

Symbolically, appearance is as important as accomplishment (Bolman and Deal 2003, pp 242–43). The political science department at this university did accomplish a lot, but appearances were not neglected. Viewed from the symbolic frame, the full-day work session looked like a carefully staged act of organizational theatre. The off-campus location was an appropriate venue. The players were given time to interact. The setting and agenda produced a very different script than is usually heard in traditional meetings and hallway conversations. The end-of-the-year party was a gala ceremony, complete with a humorous roast of a retiree and recognition for the newly tenured and promoted faculty members. Faculty members actually had some fun together.

Diane also took advantage of her knack for storytelling. She told the story of how her department reached consensus that "quality of instruction" was their top priority and that even the busiest researchers would teach at least half time. Diane boasted that by making this strong commitment to teaching, her faculty won a moral victory. Diane told the story to students, university colleagues, alumni, government, and funding agencies, and anyone else who would listen. With each telling, it got better and better. By the time she wrote it for university publications, it was close to becoming a departmental saga.

Summing Up

The key question in this scenario is, "How can an academic leader convince the faculty that differences are a group responsibility?" This is a question that deans and department chairs ask themselves over and over again. Diane's multi-frame understanding of her organization furnished an effective set of strategies for persuading faculty members to accept responsibility for departmental divisiveness. Once the faculty shouldered this burden, they were ready and able to work through their differences and reach consensus.

Chapter 5

Resources

Stepping Up to Cutbacks

NOT DECIDING IS A DECISION

Tom Roberts felt he was in the middle of a recurring nightmare when he met with the provost to hear about next year's budget. Tom served as dean of liberal arts for a large, comprehensive university on the east coast. The provost wasted no time in telling him, "I'm afraid I have some very upsetting news. The legislature has slashed university budgets. The president and I are sick about this. We both believe that the only equitable way to make cuts is for everyone to take their fair share. For our campus, we have assigned a proportional, 'across the board,' reduction of 5 percent to each college." Seeing Tom's dismay when he looked at the bottom line of his college's budget, the provost quickly pointed out, "Like every other dean on campus, Tom, you have considerable flexibility in deciding where cuts should be taken within your own college. It's in your hands."

The provost commiserated with Tom, telling him she understood his pain. "Both the president and I have started meeting with the central administrative staff. As much as we hate to do it, we're going to have to lay off our newest and youngest staff members. Every one of us involved in this process is hurting. The higher education trustees agonized over the decision to raise tuition. They know that many students in our state won't be able to go to college. I'd do anything to avoid dumping this on the deans, but at this point, we really have no choice. We must balance the budget."

Tom felt that further protests would be ignored and only convince the provost that he felt incapable of leading his college through difficult times. In truth, he did have qualms about his ability to handle angry students, staff, and faculty when they realized the impact the budget cuts would have on their lives. Tom dreaded the turmoil as faculty and staff members fought over where to make the cuts. Times of plenty were easier.

Knowing other universities in the system were going through the same tumult, Tom called a few of his colleagues to find out how they were planning to handle the cutbacks. He learned that a couple of deans had already decided to freeze faculty and staff searches, eliminate travel funds, and cancel professional development workshops. Others planned to let part-time faculty members go, postpone buying equipment, and defer maintenance on laboratories and computer facilities. Tom put together a list of these strategies.

A week after meeting with the provost, Tom brought his department chairs together to pass on the bad news and to assign them responsibility for making cuts in their departmental budgets. When Tom announced the 5 percent cut, most of the chairs were not surprised. The rumor mill bursts with hearsay during a budget crisis. What the chairs did not know, and Tom failed to clue them in earlier, was that the president and provost had allocated "across the board," proportional cuts. They were not happy to hear that Tom had agreed that proportional cuts were the only "fair" way to reduce the budget.

Tom distributed a budget projection summary identifying the dollar amount each department would be reduced, along with his suggested list of cost-cutting strategies. "You now know what your department's budget will be next year. I am not a micro-manger. I'll help you in any way that I can, but it's your job to work with your faculty and staff to decide how your budget will absorb the cut. You know much better than I do how to minimize the damage."

The chair of the History Department heatedly objected. She reminded the dean that the History Department had recently been rated top in the state. "It simply doesn't make sense to disregard quality when making decisions about expenditure cuts," she complained. "Tom, your strategy of 'across-the-board' proportional cuts is going to reduce quality all over. Do you realize what this will do to my faculty's morale after working so hard to become the state's number one History Department?"

Tom responded defensively that he felt all departments in liberal arts were top-notch. "If it was up to me, you'd all get a 5 percent increase. Unfortunately, I'm not in charge. All I can do is try to be fair in a terrible situation. Sharing the pain equally is the only way to be impartial."

The chair of the Journalism Department exploded, "Tom, you've made this decision unilaterally. Don't you think you should have consulted with the faculty, staff, and students? Perhaps you could have come up with a better alternative."

Tom replied. "It's in your hands now. You can consult with anyone you wish. I've tried to help by giving you this list of ways that other colleges like ours are reducing expenditures. Notice that none of these strategies cut any full-time faculty or staff members. That's important to me. "

After a thirty-second scan of the list, a couple of the chairs complained that the ideas looked all too familiar. "C'mon Tom," the Foreign Languages Department chair scolded, "we've all been there and done that. We're not exactly new at this. Some of us can remember the reductions in the early 1990s, and most of us suffered through the recession of 2001–2003. We're still hurting from the cuts we made back then. All these strategies are short term. When we get hit again in a year or two, what are we going to do then?"

"She's right, Tom," the English Department chair affirmed. "Take a look at this list. You've come up with potential cuts that will save most jobs, except of course, the part-time faculty positions. They have no clout anyway, right? But we'll pay a high price for laying them off. In fact, if we freeze searches, we're going to need more, not fewer faculty members. Cutting part-timers will reduce the number of sections and courses we can offer. Students won't be able to complete their degrees on time. We'll have to substantially decrease the number of students we admit next year. I can just hear parents howl."

Tom felt his face getting hot and fought to control his temper. "Let 'em howl," he said. "Maybe the legislature will hear them and restore our funding. I'm sick and tired of hearing we have to 'cut the fat.' What 'fat?' We're all working 50–60 hour weeks now. Let's stop fighting one another and channel our anger into putting pressure on the legislature. I'll be happy to go to the state capitol with you to fight that fight. Right now, though, we have to worry about next year. Please give me your department's expenditure projections for next year before our winter break. That gives you almost three months to work on it. Thank you for your help. This meeting is adjourned."

Over the next few months the college started to look like a war zone. Meetings degenerated into bitch sessions. Hallways were venues for grumbling and shouting. Friendships of twenty years were destroyed. A couple of department chairs resigned and a few younger faculty members applied for jobs in other universities.

Tom pretty much left the department chairs and faculty members alone as they worked on their budgets. When the deadline came, half of the chairs failed to turn in their expenditure projections. Tom had to explain the delay to the provost and was taken aback when she scolded: "Tom, you're the dean. It's up to you to give me your college's budget. If I don't hear from you by next Monday, I'll make the cuts myself."

Tom warned the delaying chairs that unless they submitted their budgets the provost would make cuts without their input. Reluctantly, they turned in their recommendations. Working over the weekend, Tom's heart sank when he realized that most of the chairs failed to do a credible job. Many cut their lower-division, general education courses to save resources for their own majors. Others deliberately chose to downsize their most popular programs. They hoped that the administration would bail out them out in order to avoid dealing with the flack from parents and students. Still others didn't quite meet the bottom line of reducing their budgets by 5 percent. Tom reluctantly sent them on to the provost. He knew that she would be furious and doubted that his tenure as dean would continue much longer.

VICTORY THROUGH VISION

On the other side of the country, another liberal arts dean was about to face the same problem. Gary knew that the news could not be good when the provost invited him to lunch at the faculty club. She never did that. In fact, she was known to eat her fat-free yogurt alone at her desk every day. As soon as they ordered, a garden salad for her and a cheeseburger with fries for him, Shelia got to the point.

"Gary, I hate to be the bearer of sad news, but I'm afraid we've got to prepare for cutbacks in next year's budget. The president got the word from the chancellor last week that we're looking at a 5 percent reduction. We agreed that the only fair way to make the cuts is 'across the board' reductions of 5 percent at each college."

Gary choked on a fry, and groaned, "Not again! When you add inflation, Shelia, you're really talking about more like a 10 percent cut. Look Shelia, it's too late for us to try and shave a little here and a little there. We're stretched about as thin as we can be without snapping. If we keep this up, we'll end up not doing anything very well. I think we're way over-extended in the number of programs we offer. Over the past decade alone, we've added five new master's degree programs and two new doctoral ones. They drain a lot of money for a small number of students. Maybe this is our chance to take another look at these programs. Just think of what we could do if we made undergraduate education our top priority."

"Gary, you're going to get clobbered if you hit graduate programs," Shelia warned. "Some of our super-star faculty members are here only to teach grad classes or because they need research assistants."

"I just don't think it's worth it, Shelia. I'm so weary of hearing about 'prestige.' The other day the head of the sociology department assured me that the reputation of her department is on the way up. I almost said, 'Right, you're twenty-fifth in the country and maybe, with more resources, you can get to be twenty-fourth.' Give me a break. I don't think we should pretend that our mission is to compete with Cal and Stanford."

"Gary, I'll support you and I know the president will too. The quality of this university depends largely upon the general education classes your college offers to undergraduates. But, Lord, you're going up against the big guns in your college. They're used to getting their own way. Be careful!"

With Shelia's warning ringing in his ears, Gary went back to his office and jotted down some points he wanted to make at the next college meeting. He knew that everyone would have heard about the budget reduction before the meeting and there would be a lot of worried folks.

The next day Gary met with his administrative team to try out some ideas and listen to their thoughts. Within a week, he called a meeting of all the faculty and staff in the college. Gary passed along the information about the 5 percent reduction and the president and provost's decision to do across-the-board, proportional cuts.

"I'd like us to take a different approach," Gary announced. "I think we need to set some priorities. For too long, our college has tried to be all things to all people. We no longer have that luxury. It's time to set the direction of our college."

Hearing someone sigh, "Here we go again," Gary reacted. "I know, I know, you think you've been through this before. But, let's face it folks, our mission statement and strategic plan are not much help when we need to make tough decisions. They're long on platitudes and short on practical guidelines. We need to take a fresh look at the niche our programs fill. Also, we need to honestly assess their quality. Until we do this, we don't have any basis for deciding where we should make the cuts in next year's budget."

A senior faculty member voiced the concerns of many. "Hey, Gary, this is a can of worms. What criteria are we going to use to rate our programs and who is going to be involved?"

"Good questions," Gary replied. "Let me take the last one first. All of you need to have a voice, but there are too many of us to get the job done efficiently and effectively as a large group. Our administrative team agreed that short-term task forces are the way to go. Each task force will be composed of faculty, staff, students, and alumni.

"So how do we get on a task force? Are you planning to appoint the members?" asked a skeptical faculty member.

Gary replied, "No, certainly not. In order for you all to have confidence in the task forces, you need to select your representatives. This shouldn't be too difficult. I've got nomination forms that I can give you today. We will use the structures we have in place to elect task force members. Each department will select faculty members to represent them. The staff council can choose their representatives, the student clubs will elect student reps, and I'll invite the college's alumni association to appoint representatives."

A psychology professor shot his hand up. "Hey, you haven't said anything about how many representatives are going to be involved from each department. We've got the biggest department in the college. I hope you plan to take that into account."

"Since the 'coin of the realm' in our state universities is student credit hours, of course we took size into account," Gary said. "We'll look at number of majors and minors as well as student credit hours generated in every degree program."

At the back of the room, one of the college's best-known researchers stood up. "I can't believe this," he fumed. "You know very well that those of us teaching graduate students are going to suffer by this formulation. All you're doing is 'measuring the measureables.' There are other more important considerations."

"Of course there are," Gary said. "And that gets us back to the question about criteria for assessing our programs. We propose that one task force examine the internal and external demand for all of our programs. We need another to focus on the quality of our programs. A third task force is required to look at important but more nebulous factors like program distinctiveness and contribution to the university's mission. Taken together the three task forces will give me the comprehensive input I'll need in order to make informed decisions."

"Let me make one thing clear at the outset," Gary added. "The task forces are advisory. They will not make the decisions about where we cut the budget. That's my job. That's what I get the big bucks for. Hey, that was supposed to be funny. But, seriously, I need as much input as I can in order to make informed decisions. I'll make sure that you have a chance to review and react to the task force reports. Once the reports are written, I'll schedule open hearings. All of you and all our students, staff members, and alumni will have an opportunity to be heard. I promise you that I will carefully study every bit of information the task forces give me."

Gary continued, "I hope that we will have several good candidates for the task forces. I can't imagine a more critical service to our college than serving on them. Please be thinking about who would be good task force members and encourage them to run. By the way, don't be shy about nominating yourself."

In the next few days, Gary recruited nominees for the task forces. He targeted a few younger faculty members who worried that the college's "superstars" would vote against their tenure. Gary also encouraged some senior faculty members who complained that the "researchers" treated them like "second-class citizens." As the nomination forms came in, Gary checked to see that undergraduate programs were represented by well-respected, articulate spokespeople. When he saw a gap, he got on the phone

During the time task forces met, Gary orchestrated a number of events to highlight undergraduate education. He brought in major donors to meet with faculty members. The donors were successful alumni who had completed their baccalaureate degrees in the College of Liberal Arts. They extolled the benefits of their undergraduate programs. The lead articles in the college's newsletter profiled grateful undergraduates from low-income backgrounds. Gary initiated a fall-term graduation ceremony for undergraduates and asked all faculty members to attend.

When the reports of each task force came in, the message was clear: undergraduate programs were more valuable to the college than graduate programs. On almost every criterion, undergraduate education came out on top. Demand was higher, quality was better, programs were more central to the university mission, and, not insignificantly, costs were lower.

The faculty was not surprised. Gary had shared the task force reports with everyone and listened to arguments in favor and against their findings in open hearings. After announcing his recommendations to phase out some grad programs and cut back on others, Gary met individually with department chairs and faculty members in all programs that were affected. He found these one-on-one meetings with chairs and faculty members to be the most difficult stage of the process. Gary had to make the case that the college could not afford to keep their programs alive. Reactions ranged from quiet disappointment to loud outrage.

Along with cuts to graduate programs, Gary also recommended substantial reductions in his office. He froze the search to replace a retiring associate dean, eliminated a vacant clerical position in his office, and cut back his travel plans. Gary knew that these cuts would hurt, but felt it was crucial to show the faculty that he was bearing some of the burden.

In his preface to the college's recommendations, Gary praised the task force members and said, "Thanks to the work of the task forces and the input of many other faculty and staff members, students, and alumni, our college has hammered out a clear mission. Our number one priority is providing our undergraduates with an excellent education. Although cutting the budget is always difficult, together we reaffirmed the values of fairness, civility, and professionalism that characterize our college's culture."

VIEWING THE VICTIM AND THE VICTOR: A COMPREHENSIVE ANALYSIS

In a delightful, tongue-in-cheek piece, "The Dean of Happiness: Why Bad Times Are Good," Dean Stanley Fish proclaimed that it is much "easier" to be a dean in hard times because everyone expects you to say "no."

When the money disappears, there are no decisions to make, and as long as you breathe the right combination of regret ("Gee, I wish I could") and hope ("Wait until next year") and don't publicly criticize your superiors, you will smell like a rose and everyone will love you and praise you for managing so well in hard times (Fish, 2003, p. 5).

Deans struggling with the same problems that Tom and Gary faced would probably disagree that "bad times are good." And we're talking about most deans in American universities. "Scarcity" has become a "way of life" for universities in the 21st century (Tierney, 1998, p. 2). That's the bad news.

The good news is that a decline in resources does not automatically decrease quality and effectiveness. When Cameron and Smart (1998) examined the organizational effectiveness of universities with declining resources, they discovered that over half of these universities were doing just fine. They found that the "way in which downsizing and decline occur is more important than that they occur" (p. 83). Even more heartening for deans and chairs was their discovery that good managers can prevent the major predictors of ineffectiveness (p. 81). Cameron and Smart called them "the dirty dozen." They include:

- Short-term crisis mentality
- Loss of innovativeness
- Resistance to change
- Decreasing morale
- Politicized interest groups
- Non-prioritized cutbacks
- Loss of trust
- Increasing conflict
- Restricted communication
- Lack of teamwork
- Scapegoating leaders
- Centralization

(Cameron and Smart, 1998, p. 81)

Leadership Lessons

This list of characteristics reads like a profile of Tom's college. Let's take a brief look aided by the four frames to see why Tom got pelted with the "dirty dozen" and how Gary deftly dodged them. As we examine their behavior, we identify lessons for deans and chairs going through budget cutbacks.

Don't "Pass the Buck"—Especially in Hard Times

Gary knew he was the college's leader and acted accordingly. Faculty members were grateful that Gary accepted responsibility for recommending the budget cuts in their college to the provost. His structural perspective helped him see that making tough decisions is what deans are paid to do. Tom, on the other hand, did not seem to know his place in the formal chain of command. He understood well enough that the department chairs reported to him and he reported to the provost, but he refused to accept the responsibility that the provost had delegated to him. Instead, Tom "passed the buck." Passing the buck is never a good strategy. In a crisis, it is disastrous.

As Tom found out, relinquishing administrative control does not mean that faculty or students assume control. It means that there is no control. Plante and Caret (1990) warn that when leaders shirk responsibility, "The center will simply not hold" (p. 114). Although universities are supposedly among the most democratic of organizations, during times of budget reductions, they become increasingly hierarchical (Zussman, 1999, p. 117). And, this is not necessarily a bad thing. Atwell and Green (1985, p. 189) point out, "The more perilous the situation, the more the collegiate community needs and welcomes strong leadership."

Capitalize on Budget Cutbacks to Promote your Goals

Gary understood that there is more pressure on the faculty to prioritize during a budget crisis. He turned the budget reduction challenge into what Massey (1996) calls, "a target of opportunity" (p. 25.) Instead of "nickel and dimeing" it, Gary set an agenda—improving undergraduate education. First, he made sure the provost and president were on board. Next, he built support for the agenda by recruiting like-minded faculty members to serve on the task forces. A consummate political leader, Gary did not try to avoid conflict. Rather, he managed conflict by establishing the task forces, holding open hearings, and meeting with individuals most affected by the cutbacks.

Gary experienced less resistance than he had expected. There were many cheerleaders for improving undergraduate programs. In fact, most of his faculty was relieved to support a dean that pushed values other than high-profile research. Because faculty members trusted Gary and many agreed with him, morale stayed high.

Tom's failure to understand the political realities of the situation left power up for grabs and fomented conflict. Tom feared that the budget reduction process would lead to confrontations with faculty members, students, and parents. He dreaded having to deal with conflict. The irony is that there was considerably more conflict in Tom's college than in Gary's: friendships were damaged, department chairs resigned, and faculty members looked for positions in other universities.

Establish Frequent Two-way Communication and Share the Burden

Tom doesn't look any better in the human resources frame than he did in the political frame. Tom isolated himself. As a result, trust was eroded and morale suffered. Gary's actions responded to needs we all share. We want to know what's going on. Gary communicated with all stakeholders. Everyone wants to feel that his or her opinions are valued. Gary listened. He understood that one of the best ways to increase productivity and raise morale was to encourage participation. Another human resources strategy Gary used was taking more than his share of the burden. Gary froze the search for an associate dean and reduced clerical support and travel money for his office.

Broadcast your Agenda

Gary's symbolic leadership was every bit as strong. He was visible and accessible. Gary schmoozed with faculty members—especially those whom he thought would favor undergraduate programs. Through newsletters, events for undergraduates, and meetings with donors, the faculty heard a compelling story about the centrality of undergraduate education. Handpicked students, alumni, and donors broadcast that message; the fall graduation ceremony celebrated it. Gary reaffirmed the college's "culture of civility and professionalism."

Summing Up

Tom's basic problem was his narrow view of the deanship. Structurally, he limited his options to only one—delegating. Tom's fear of conflict cut off political strategies. His isolation precluded human resource and symbolic efforts. Gary's multi-frame perspective generated a variety of good options. He demonstrated that reframing is a powerful tool to design elastic strategies. Gary combined hardheaded realism with a passionate commitment to a larger value. But we need to clarify a major point. When we concluded that Gary relied on all four lenses, we did not mean that he looked at each sequentially. Gary's strength was that he saw his situation *simultaneously from the standpoint of structural clarity, human needs, political realities, and cultural values.* (Bolman and Deal, 2003, p.433). Gary modeled multi-frame thinking—the capacity to think in several ways at the same time about the same thing.

In the next chapter we apply multi-frame thinking to the dean's relationship with the provost.

Chapter 6

Bosses

Winning over the Higher-Ups

HAVING YOUR SAY, NOT YOUR WAY

"Who the hell does she think she is?" fumed George Lujan to a fellow dean. George had just learned that the provost turned down a faculty member he had recommended for tenure and promotion. "She's been here the grand total of six months and managed to screw up our budget, scare away our students, and demoralize our faculty. I'm so damn sick of having to spend my life trying to educate new provosts. Do you realize she's the third provost we've had in the past five years?"

"Hey, take it easy," his colleague admonished. "She's not that bad. In fact, I feel pretty positive. I think she has an enormous job and is doing the best she can. I like her!"

"Well, of course, you do," George grumbled. "She loves the liberal arts. In her heart, the provost believes that professors belong in libraries writing esoteric articles for refereed journals. Well, that just doesn't cut it in the School of Social Work or, for that matter, in any professional school. We've got to have faculty members working in the community with practitioners. If we don't, we can say 'good-bye' to field placements for our students and jobs for our graduates. First, she cut our funds for supervising field placements. Now, she's turned down one of my best faculty members. He's done more to build the reputation of our school with social workers than anyone. I'm just sick about this."

"George, George, George, you're asking for a heart attack. If you feel so strongly, you need to meet with the provost to explain your case. She's a reasonable woman. Give her a chance."

Acting on his colleague's advice, George made an appointment to see Provost Ann Wilcox. He started the meeting by saying, "Thanks for meeting with me, Ann. I know how busy you are. Ten years ago, when I came here, I thought that first year would never end. I wouldn't have bothered you if I didn't feel so strongly about your decision not to back my recommendation for Juan's tenure and promotion."

The provost responded. "Frankly George, I was very disappointed that you supported his application. I spent quite a bit of time with his file. As far as I could see, he's only published two articles in the past five years. Neither of them appeared in the top journals in your field. I can see he's been active on the local scene, but I didn't notice that he's held any positions within national associations or even made any presentations at the state or national level. Did I miss something?"

George exploded, "You sure did! I knew when you cut our supervision budget that you didn't understand what our school needs. Getting out in the real world helping real people is the critical experience for our students. We depend a lot more on faculty members who have credibility with social workers than we do on faculty members who publish articles that nobody reads. I know most of the social workers in the area. They think Juan is a superstar. He came to us after working for over a decade in Child Protective Services. He can 'walk the walk' as well as 'talk the talk.' As dean, I believe that building good relations with the field is one of my most important responsibilities. More than any other member of my faculty, Juan has helped me do this."

"OK, George, you've told me about your most important responsibility. Let me tell you about mine. The president hired me to 'get this place on the map' and I aim to do just that. We're way behind other comparable universities in getting research funds. We have fewer applications to graduate programs. Our faculty applicant pools are not as strong. If we want to compete successfully for dollars and top new faculty members and students, we must upgrade our faculty.

"I realize that I'm not going to win any popularity contests enforcing higher standards for faculty members, but that's not my job. If university leaders don't enforce high standards, who will? I expected faculty committees to approve borderline applications for tenure and promotion, but I thought our deans would appreciate and support what I'm trying to do. Guess you don't."

"It's not a question of supporting or not supporting you," George fired back, "My job is to support the School of Social Work. And I've done that pretty well over the past ten years, if you put any credence in our accrediting agency. I know how to improve the quality of our school."

"Glad to hear it," Ann replied, "and I know how to improve the quality of our university. You don't do that by retaining and promoting faculty members who can't measure up. You can argue all you want that Juan meets your school's criteria, but university criteria takes precedence over any school or department's priorities. If it didn't work that way, we wouldn't have a university. We would have a loose collection of independent feudal baronies."

"Under the banner of centralized authority, do you have any idea what you're doing to faculty morale on this campus?" George asked. "Don't you realize how unfair it is for you to come in and autocratically change all the rules within a few months? I know that Juan is not the only faculty member in our professional schools who you've turned down. These people have worked hard for the last five years to be good teachers. They've provided excellent service to their departments, schools, and to the wider professional community. Now you're punishing them for doing just what the university asked them to do."

Ann said, "C'mon George. You're the one who is not being fair. I'm not autocratically imposing new rules. University-wide criteria are traditionally based on teaching, service, *and* scholarship. The fact is that scholarship has been largely overlooked here until now. I can see by your reaction that I'm getting the message out that this oversight has come to an end. No, George, I will not reconsider my decision on Juan's tenure and promotion. I'm sorry, but the president is waiting for me now. I need to go."

Getting up from the table, George fired his last salvo: "You provosts come and go through a revolving door. That's not the sad thing. What's sad is that while you're here, you drive out good faculty members and leave us holding the bag."

DEALING WITH NEW BOSSES: AN ANALYSIS

We have sympathy for George. Many deans we know complain about the rapid turnover of provosts and presidents in their universities. In an informal survey we conducted a few years ago, this was listed in the top five "most pressing problems" by 50 percent of our deans. So what can deans do other than blow up at new provosts who fail to support them?

Leadership Lessons

Take Time to Educate the Boss

George said he was tired of "educating" the provost. That's too bad for George because in our judgment, one of the dean's most important jobs is to "educate" the provost. This job is especially crucial when a new provost comes on board. George waited too long to present his case about the special needs of the School of Social Work. He should have had that conversation, minus its argumentative tone, when the provost first came on board. By the time of this meeting it was too late. The provost had already cut funds for field experiences and turned down Juan's application for tenure and promotion.

"Educating" a new provost takes more than just meetings. George Lujan missed a good opportunity to get his message across by exercising his symbolic leadership skills. At the beginning of the academic year, his school invites the supervisors of the school's social work interns to attend an orientation session and reception. George could have invited the provost to attend. Even better, he might have asked her to speak at the gathering. Ann would have learned something about the cohesive culture of George's school. By introducing her to the social work supervisors, Ann could have a specific face or two in mind when George spoke about field supervision. Ann probably would have thanked the supervisors and said some nice words about how important they are to the university. Provosts can usually be counted on to say these kinds of things to the community. That's part of their jobs.

Find Allies among Other Deans

Bolman and Deal (2006) call effective political leaders "warriors." Warriors don't win wars by fighting battles they cannot win. Generals cannot win battles if they don't have a plan and if they don't have any allies. Political leaders build support networks for their agendas. George acted, or rather, reacted alone.

Who might have helped George? Well, for a start, how about his fellow deans of professional schools in the university? George said that the provost's policies were detrimental to all professional schools. Had the deans of nursing, education, and social work come together, they could have been a formidable political force. Their students and alumni are typically sizable. Many faculty members in professional schools form close ties with their colleagues in the community. Teachers, nurses, and social workers agree that "real life experiences in the trenches" are the most valuable part of their professional training. They appreciate college professors who take the trouble to get to know them on their own turf. When deans of professional schools successfully harness their collective power, few provosts or presidents can safely ignore them.

Bolster your Case with Policy Reports and Research

If you think this political route sounds too subversive, let's shift to the structural frame and look at the potential impact of relevant policy reports and research. For example, the changes in promotion and tenure criteria recommended by Ernest Boyer in the Carnegie Foundation for the Advancement of

Teaching report, *Scholarship Reconsidered: Priorities of the Professoriate* (1990), could have helped George make his case. The report touched off a firestorm about expanding criteria for promotion and tenure. Many universities have since revised promotion and tenure guidelines incorporating expectations for faculty members to meet community needs. Had George related examples of top-notch universities that have expanded their criteria to reward professional service and outreach (see Rice and Sorcinelli, 2002, pp. 110–13 for examples), Ann might have listened. At the very least, George would have recast the discussion about scholarship criteria in terms more favorable to his school. Of course this conversation needed to happen before she started reviewing applications for promotion and tenure.

Give Care that Makes a Difference

We refer to human resources leaders as "care-givers." We do not doubt for a moment that George did care about Juan's future at the university, and that he probably cared for Juan personally. But implicit in the concept of a human resources leader is that the caring must be truly helpful. George's care of Juan was not.

What kinds of caring could have made George more helpful? Deans and department chairs who have a good track record of getting their probationary faculty members through the tenure and promotion process make sure candidates clearly understand the criteria and provide psychological as well as financial support to help them meet the criteria (e.g., assigned time for research, travel funds to present at conferences, money for research assistants). Deans and chairs meet at least annually with the candidates to assess progress. If there is a problem, the dean and chair make sure the candidate understands what needs to be done and tries to help him or her get back on track. This is care-giving that makes a difference and minimizes surprises to probationary faculty members. Gunsalus (2006) suggests that "no surprises" ought to be the university administrator's "mantra" when evaluating faculty members (p. 219).

Summing Up

What can we learn from this scenario? If we had to choose just one lesson it would be, "Do not alienate your provost!" The provost is one person in the university the dean must get along with. The "critical feature of academic life" for faculty members may be "the absence of a boss" as Rosovsky (1990, p.163) maintained, but deans do have a boss. The boss is the provost, sometimes called the academic vice-president. Deans serve "at the pleasure of the president." That usually means, at the "pleasure of the provost." Don't underestimate the importance of the university structure and be sure you understand your place in it.

What the structural frame does not reveal is that in the provost's eyes you are the embodiment of your school or college. You need to view your iconic position symbolically to appreciate that you are not just the leader, spokesperson, or representative for your college. You are the college. If you have a good relationship with your provost, faculty members and students in your college will benefit. If you do not, they will suffer. In this scenario, Juan and his students bore the brunt of George's failure to play all his cards to influence the provost.

On a brighter note, let's follow the progress of another professional school dean who wants to win her reluctant provost's support for an innovative program.

TAKING THE LEAD

Carol Atkins, dean of the College of Business, was worried. Enrollments in the MBA program were shrinking and so were alumni donations. Over the past few years, four large biotech firms had moved to the region. That they had not hired any of Carol's graduates, nor showed interest in collaborating with her college, added to Carol's worries.

Carol contacted one of the CEOs and learned that he had recently brought on board several graduates of Professional Science Master's (PSM) programs from other universities. He told Carol that graduates from PSM programs had the kinds of background and skills they were looking for. "Carol, in our industry we need people trained in both science and business; employees who can make good, data-based decisions. Your MBAs don't have the science background that we need and the science grads lack business skills. Let me know if your university ever gets it act together to start a Professional Science Master's program. I'd be willing to help and I know that you could count on other folks in this business to participate." Carol promised that she would get back to him within the week.

As soon as Carol hung up the phone, she called Larry Krug, the science dean in her university and asked if she could visit with him that day. Before their appointment, she checked the Internet to learn more about the content of PSM programs and funding sources. When she got to Larry's office, she was pumped.

"Larry, you've heard of Professional Science Master's programs?" Seeing him nod in the affirmative, Carol declared: "Well, I think our university should offer one. We can provide your students with the business background they need to get hired by biotech firms right here in the city. And, I'm almost certain that we can get industry buy-in and start-up funds. I just checked into the possibility of start-up funds from the Sloan Foundation. Thanks to them, universities all across the country have initiated PSM degree programs."

Larry reacted positively. "That's quite a big proposal for a Friday afternoon, Carol. You've got my attention. I have heard from colleagues on other campuses that their PSM programs have caused enrollment to mushroom in biology and chemistry. Many of their top graduates go right on to get their master's degree in the PSM program. They say that PSM alumni pull down great jobs. No wonder. Their starting salaries are twice as much as we pay our new professors with PhDs. They can't produce enough graduates to meet the demand."

"I'd be willing to work with you to start our own PSM program," Larry went on, "but I really don't think Dennis will support it. You know how conservative our provost is. Lately he's vetoed everything that might cost the university money. I don't know if you are aware that a million years ago, Dennis was a biology professor. He's an absolute stickler for protecting the so-called 'academic integrity' of science programs. Between you and me, what Dennis really is concerned about is protecting their turf. Dennis is from the 'old school.' He really thinks universities ought to be insulated from the pressures of the outside world. Besides, he's getting to be a crotchety, old fart."

Laughing, Carol agreed that it wouldn't be easy to get a green light from the provost. "But, it's a worth a try," she affirmed. "We know that the provost's eyes are always on the bottom line. If we can convince him that this program will bring in more donations from both industry and future alumni, he just might be persuaded—particularly if we can get start-up funds and it doesn't cost the university a cent. Besides, the president would love the publicity. Just think of his "Friend Raising is Fund Raising" campaign. We could connect the president to new friends, wealthy friends, in the biotech companies. Already, I can picture him in his golf togs plastered all over the local papers with his new CEO buddies on the eighteenth green."

"Okay, Carol, what do we have to lose? I'll check with a few of our faculty's hot shots to find out if they'd be interested in participating. If they buy in, the provost might have more confidence that the new program will set high standards. Would you contact some business faculty members? Also, why not check back with your CEO contact to see if he can recruit some other industry supporters."

"I'll call him right away, Larry. Wouldn't it be neat if he could get a couple of 'high-rollers' to call our president? I think the provost would be much more agreeable if the president is in our camp."

In the next week, Carol called the CEO to give him a progress report. He promised that he would drum up support from other companies and personally call the president. He also pledged to raise money to refurbish and equip a laboratory at the university, if the PSM program gained approval.

In preparation for meeting with the provost, Carol reviewed his annual goals and was pleased to learn that launching a PSM program was directly related to his goals of augmenting annual giving, increasing enrollment in graduate programs, and improving the quality of science laboratories. She called the Sloan Foundation for an application for PSM start-up funds. When Larry and Carol met with the provost, they were ready.

Carol led off. "My daughter just loves singing alto in the choir with your granddaughter. Is she heading here for college next year?" After a few minutes of chitchat, Larry decided they heard enough bragging about the provost's granddaughter and intervened.

"Dennis, we're here to get your OK to design a Professional Science Master's program. Carol has done a lot of research about PSM programs, and I think you'll be interested in hearing what they've done for universities that currently offer them. She's also contacted local CEOs in the biotech industry who want to help us. We've both talked with faculty members and identified some strong participants. I am sold on the idea. We're ready to get started on our planning. We want to assure you at the outset that we are not asking for any money from the university."

Carol took the floor, hitting points in line with the provost's goals. When he raised concerns about protecting academic standards, Larry told him that two biology professors, known for their high standards and academic rigor, had signed on to write the proposal. When he asked about financial commitments, Carol informed him that she and Larry wanted to apply for start-up funds from the Sloan Foundation.

"I've talked with a few business deans in universities with PSM programs," Carol said. "They say that PSM alumni and their partner-businesses have donated heavily to their universities. After all, many PSM graduates go into well-paid management jobs. I guess it's not surprising that they have more high-quality applicants than they know what to do with."

The provost sighed and smiled ruefully, "Well, you two have certainly done your homework. I got a call from the president this morning asking me to support you in any way that I could. Seems he thinks we can get one of our labs remodeled and fully equipped with the latest technology."

At this point, Dennis sat up very straight and looking directly at Carol said, "Still, I'm not completely convinced. I've yet to see a new program that didn't cost the university a lot of money to get off the ground. But I have other concerns besides money. I don't like to think that our university will become primarily a vocational institution. Education is about more than getting a well-paying job. I need to know more about the kind of curriculum you plan to develop before I could give a go-ahead. Also, you'd have to find out if you can recruit business representatives in our community willing to devote the time and effort needed to get this program up and running. You say there are a few faculty members interested in the program, but do you have enough of the ones you need? What about interest among students? You said yourself, Carol, that there are a lot of successful PSM programs out there. What's to keep our science graduates from going to an established program in another university or taking one of the over a hundred PSM programs on-line? See, I did some homework, too."

Carol and Larry sat quietly and listened as Dennis aired his concerns. When he was finished, Carol said, "I appreciate that you took the time to look up information about PSM degree programs. You raise some very good points, Dennis. Let's make sure that Larry and I fully understand them. You need assurance that our PSM program will meet high standards. You want to know about the curriculum of the program and the level of student interest. You want to make sure that there are enough faculty members and business representatives who are willing and able to plan and operate a PSM degree program. And, you want to know where the money is coming from to launch it. Does that cover what you said?"

Dennis replied that it did. Carol concluded the meeting by saying, "I think that, together, Larry and I can address your concerns, but we'll need a little time. How about we put our request for your approval to design the program on hold for now? We'd like to get back to you in a few months time?"

"I'll agree to an exploratory period," Dennis conceded, "but I want to set an appointment for a progress report in six months." Carol asked if the provost would object if she sent him information about PSM programs from time to time. "Sure, Carol, I'll try to review what you send me, but please make your epistles brief." They thanked the provost and went back to Carol's office to plan their campaign.

Carol and Larry spent the next six months recruiting faculty members, surveying potential students, meeting with industry representatives and visiting successful PSM programs. They organized a small group of faculty and industry "cheerleaders" to help them write a proposal to fund planning of their PSM program. Of course, all these activities had to be sandwiched in around their already busy schedules. They were stretched pretty thin, but the enthusiasm of the participants energized them.

Carol prepared several one-page information summaries to educate the provost about PSM programs. In one background piece, she explained that central issues facing both universities and business triggered the impetus for the new degree program: intense competition in the business world, the global economy, technological advances, and the convergence of academic and professional fields of knowledge (National Research Council of the National Academies, 2008 pp. 9–15). She suggested that higher education and businesses could help each other deal with these issues. In another, she contrasted the poor employment prospects for science PhDs with the excellent offers given to PSM graduates and passed along one expert's assessment that, "The streamlined, targeted, real-world master's degree is beginning to elbow the fabled doctorate off academia's center stage" (Hartington, 2002, p. 6).

Most of the summaries that Carol sent to the provost focused on the concerns he raised at their meeting and on his annual goals. To address the issue of curriculum substance and rigor, Carol forwarded to the provost a few curriculum outlines of top PSM programs as well as a copy of the standards set by the Council of Graduate Schools that programs must meet. Carol asked her colleague business deans for data showing donations from industry and alumni to the university before and after PSM programs were established and e-mailed the results to the provost. She surveyed current science students and reported the substantial number indicating interest in a PSM program on campus. Carol sent Dennis an updated list of faculty members and industry representatives committed to work together on the new program.

Carol and Larry started off their six-month progress report to the provost with big news. The university won a start-up grant from the Sloan Foundation to design a PSM program. Over the past six months, Carol and Larry had recruited a team of enthusiastic business representatives and faculty members to plan the new curriculum. They were ready to hire a program coordinator who had industry and university experience. Carol reviewed the names of business and faculty representatives willing to serve on a new PSM Industry Advisory Board and asked the provost if he would participate. She also mentioned that the president had asked her if he could address the board at its first meeting.

Dennis told the deans, "I must admit that I had some real reservations about us getting into this program when you first brought it up. Now, I'm excited to be a part of it. Of course, I'll be happy to serve on the Industry Advisory Board. If this program looks as good as I think it will, I'll help you get it through the Academic Senate and will be pleased to approve it. Good work!"

Fast-forwarding to a day in May, four-years later, the first PSM program graduates are deluged with excellent offers. Local industry has provided state-of-the-art equipment for two new labs. Thanks to donors from biotech firms, donations are way up. The president is hosting a reception for Industry Advisory Board members as well as participating faculty members and PSM graduates.

The president opens with welcoming remarks. "We are here today to thank all of you, our business partners, faculty members, and graduates for making this university's Professional Science Master's degree program such a success. I understand that twice as many qualified students applied to the program this year than we have space for. You graduates were pretty smart to come in at the beginning. I've heard about some terrific projects that you have completed under your industry mentors. You have learned about real-world problems and contributed to solving them. Good for you! Now, I'd like to call on our two deans, Carol Atkins and Larry Krug, the 'movers and shakers,' who got this program going."

Carol and Larry shared the podium. They introduced the participating faculty members, business representatives, and PSM graduates. Carol said, "If it weren't for every one, this program would not be here. Larry and I want to thank each of you for your continued support."

"Today, we're starting a new tradition. Every year we would like to recognize one individual who has made an outstanding contribution to the PSM program. As you can imagine, there were many candidates for this honor. However, one stood out. With the unanimous agreement of the Industry Advisory Board, Larry and I are pleased to present this year's first annual, Friend of the Professional Science Master's Program Award to our provost, Dennis Palmer. We wanted to be able to promise him 10 percent of the salaries our PSM graduates will earn in their first year, but our students didn't think that was a good idea. Instead, Dennis, you get a hug from me, a handshake from Larry, and this plaque to expresses our gratitude to you for championing the PSM program. On behalf of all of us here today, I want to say 'thank you.' You're the best!"

ASKING THE RIGHT QUESTIONS

The power of multiple-frame thinking is not so much in the answers it provides, but rather in the questions it generates. Being consciously aware of the four lenses guides you to ask more and better questions. This is crucial because the answers to the questions you ask determine your actions and a good share of the reactions of others. Let's take a look at the implicit questions Carol asked herself and how they are related to the four frames. Chairs as well as deans can win over their supervisors by asking these questions. We ask chairs to simply substitute the word "dean" for "provost" to make the questions Carol asked relevant to them.

Leadership Lessons

What do I Want to Accomplish?

Both Carol and George asked: "What do I want to accomplish?" The answer to this question sets the agenda, the first step in the political frame. For George, the answer was to convince the provost to change her mind about rejecting his candidate for tenure and promotion. For Carol, the answer was to win the provost's support to start a new program to prepare graduates for positions in the biotech industry. They both had an agenda, but this is where they part company.

What are the Provost's Goals, Interests, and Concerns?

Carol went on to ask, "What are the provost's goals, interests, and concerns?" She wanted to understand what would motivate the provost to support the PSM program. Carol checked on the provost's annual goals, talking with others about his interests, and, most important, listening carefully to what he had to say. In academe, listening intently is so rare a phenomenon that it is almost irresistible. The provost knew that Carol was listening to him because she repeated his concerns to make sure she understood them.

In the meeting with his provost, George sounded like he was "listening ahead," preparing his rebuttal while Ann was talking (Gunsalus, 2006, p. 72). He didn't bother with researching what the provost cared about and what she hoped to achieve. Based only on the few decisions the provost had made regarding his school, George was convinced that he already knew all he needed to know about her. George acted as if he subscribed to the adage, "It's more important to have your say than to have your way." Unfortunately for him, those who insist on having their "say," sometimes do not get their "way."

What can I Do to Win Over the Provost?

While she was gathering information about the provost, Carol addressed the question, "What can I do to win over Dennis?" Carol understood that faculty and students in the College of Business would benefit from her efforts to build a positive relationship with the provost. When we look at Carol's interaction with the provost, we see that many of her strategies overlap the frames. Was her opening chat about the provost's granddaughter coming from the human resources frame? Yes, "cultivating likeability" by establishing a "human connection" is a bedrock human resource technique. But it is also an effective political move because getting people to like you helps you recruit allies and negotiate successfully. As Gunsalus (2006) points out, "it is a fact of human nature that we give more to people we like than to people we don't like" (p. 82).

Who can Help me Gain the Provost's Support?

One of the biggest differences between Dean George Lujan and Dean Carol Atkins is that Carol began building a network of supporters before she met with her provost and continued to expand it after the meeting. Carol's answer to her question, "Who can help me gain the provost's support?" was to recruit key stakeholders. First, she converted Larry Krug, the dean of the Science College. Only Larry could respond to the some of the provost's concerns about program standards as well as generate interest from science faculty members and students. Another important advocate was the president. In fact, the president's call voicing his interest in the program may have been the critical factor in getting an initial green light from the provost. Carol brought on the business faculty and helped to enlist biotech corporate representatives to sign up for developing the PSM program.

What does the Provost Need to Know?

At the same time that Carol was responding to her question about who could help win over the provost, she also was considering another question: "What does the provost need to know to convince him to support a PSM program?"

Carol applied a good lesson from the human resources frame to combine advocacy and inquiry. She composed brief information pieces to allay the provost's anxieties about the quality of the curriculum and program standards, the extent of faculty participation and student interest, and the commitment of biotech companies. The data showing increased donations that she gathered from colleague deans who had established PSM programs made the provost salivate. He began to see Carol's long-term vision: graduates prepared to contribute to an industry essential to the American economy; more and better students in both colleges—science and business; bigger contributions of money, facilities, and equipment from industry and alumni; incentives to recruit outstanding faculty members; and expanded opportunities for other projects through the university and business partnership. Carol's campaign to "Educate Dennis" succeeded with flying colors.

How can the Provost's Support be Sustained?

Finally, another very important question Carol asked was, "How can the provost's support be sustained?" Most of Carol's questions came out of the political and human resources frame. But the structural and symbolic perspectives also influenced her. She saw that neither the university nor industry had a structure to promote and maintain partnership programs. So Carol helped establish the Industry Advisory Board to oversee the operation of the PSM program and to keep it robust.

In a flash of insight, Carol asked the provost to serve on the Industry Advisory Board. The provost's participation in the board converted him from an "outsider" to an "insider." As a member of the Industry Advisory Board, he shared responsibility for making the program a success. He became more knowledgeable about partnerships with business, expanded his reference group to include colleagues from industry, and in the process made some new friends. When the board approved Carol's nomination of the provost for their first annual "Friend of the Professional Science Master's Program Award," the provost became a true believer. It was a purely symbolic act, but it touched the provost's heart.

Summing Up

In review, we recommend that deans and chairs ask themselves the following questions when they are trying to win over the boss:

- What am I trying to accomplish?
- What are the provost's (dean's) goals, interests, and concerns (and how are they related to my agenda)?
- What can I do to win him or her over?
- Who can help me gain the provost's (dean's) support?
- What does the provost (dean) need to know?
- How can the provost's (dean's) support be sustained?

We need to point out that, despite appearances, Carol did not necessarily know more about being a dean than George did. After all, so much of our knowledge in administration is based on intuition and experience. We are convinced that most deans and chairs have the knowledge they need; they just don't know how to access it. The key is asking the right questions. You cannot formulate the right questions if you see your situation from only one or two perspectives. George's tunnel vision restricted the questions he asked and, therefore, the options he considered.

Carol demonstrated that multi-frame thinking generates a range of broad and deep questions. But this is an important point: none of her answers to any one question was remarkable. We would be surprised if other deans are unable to answer the same questions as well or better. So why was Carol so successful? Remember our definition for "multi-frame thinking": "the capacity to think in several ways at the same time about the same thing?" (Bolman and Deal, 2003, p. 433). Carol's campaign got the provost on board because she raised the right questions and worked to answer them simultaneously on all fronts.

In the following chapter, we zoom in on a new department chair as he inherits a plate full of troubles. We show how he uses all the frames to build a comprehensive understanding of what it will take to move his department ahead.

Chapter 7

The Way It's "Spozed" to Be

Leadership in Action

THE DEAN'S RANT

Jason remembered his grandfather's advice as he walked across campus after his meeting with the dean. He could almost hear the old man's gravelly voice warn, "Be careful what you ask for." Jason had wanted to be chair of the Music Department at North Central State University for as long as he could remember. Throughout his life, he had listened to his music-teacher father brag about the outstanding education he had received there. As a faculty member at another institution in the state system, Jason had been impressed by the quality of North Central's music graduates. The prospect of not only being a member of that distinguished faculty, but their leader, seemed like a dream. Now, thinking over the dean's rant, it felt more like a nightmare. That night he asked his wife, "Do you think that Barack Obama felt as desperate as I do after his first two days on the job?"

During Jason's interview six months ago, the dean had briefly mentioned that there were "some problems" in the department. Today, he dropped the whole load of bricks. "Music is the most dysfunctional department in our college, probably in the entire university. Having two lousy chairs in the past three years accelerated a downward spiral. At this point, the situation is entirely out of hand. Faculty members can't agree on anything. Whenever I run into anyone from music, all I hear is nasty gossip about someone else in the department. Oh yeah, I also hear a lot of whining. God, I'm sick of all of them. Student enrollment is down, student complaints are up, and not a damn

---

This chapter is adapted from the case of a new principal, presented by Bolman and Deal, 2003, pp. 409–430.

thing is ever turned in on time. If they don't get their act together soon they won't pass the university's program review. Let me tell you Jason, this is not the year to screw up. With the lousy economy, our budget is taking a beating. Weaker programs in the university are sure to be phased out. The Music Department is vulnerable. You've got your work cut out for you."

Jason wondered if anyone was strong enough to handle these problems. He doubted that he was. This was a new feeling for him. Jason had always felt pretty confident about his ability. He was the youngest person to be promoted to full professor in his previous institution. Like most new department chairs, he had not received any training for his job, but he thought that his experience running the college's concert series gave him some understanding of administrative tasks. In addition, Jason had been popular with his colleagues and served as chair of several important committees. He had worked closely with his former department chair preparing for their last accreditation visit. Jason was grateful that he had these experiences, but painfully aware that he had a lot to learn in a short time.

GETTING TO KNOW THEM

Jason told himself, "I've only got a week before the fall semester starts. I'd better get moving." Jason opened his office door and perched on the edge of his secretary's desk. "Hannah, I'm on a fact finding mission. You've been here over twenty years, what can you tell me about our department that can help me do a good job? I really need your input."

Two hours later, Jason went back to his office and jotted down the names of key faculty members that Hannah identified. "She sure knows where all the bodies are buried," Jason thought. "And she wasn't shy about telling me the ones she wishes were buried. Hannah knows the department's history and that's something I desperately need to learn. What happened in the past that led to the current mess?"

According to Hannah, the department is badly splintered. The performance faculty members don't mingle with the musicologists—the professors who teach music history, theory, and musicology. The performance faculty sees them as failed musicians who ended up in the classroom because they could not hack it on stage. The musicologists complain that the performers know very little about music, except about their own instrument. "The truth is," Hannah observed, "neither group knows anything much about the other. The only faculty members who seem to be able to work successfully with both are the composition faculty. If you want an unbiased view, you might talk with them."

Jason asked Hannah to schedule appointments with as many faculty members as she could within the week. He asked her to start with the ones she had identified as the "sanest member" of each of the three groups in the department.

The first one Jason interviewed was Harry Stippet, an elderly, nationally known, music historian. Harry's office was a stereotype of the absent-minded professor's lair. Books, scores, and articles spilled out of shelves. The air smelled musty, even though the windows were open to the warm summer air. Against regulations, Harry was puffing on his pipe when Jason walked in.

Jason told Harry that his text was "the Bible" of music history and said that it was "an honor" to serve on the same faculty with him. He told Harry he would appreciate hearing his views of the department's problems and assured him that anything he said would be confidential. Harry admitted that the department was in total disarray. Meetings had degenerated into name-calling and nothing was getting done. In his view, no one seemed to like coming to campus any more.

When Jason asked him why morale was so low, Harry pointed to the previous chairs. "Both of them were a disaster," he said. "They only listened to their friends. One chair, a first-rate violinist by the way, turned out to be a third-rate chair. He gave his fellow performers the best schedules, the most summer work, and the lion's share of travel money. His successor, and I'm embarrassed to tell you that she is also a music historian, showed the same kind of favoritism to us. You can just imagine what that did for departmental unity."

Jason's next appointment was with Sarah Clark, the cello instructor and an informal leader of the "performers." Sarah was a petite woman in her mid-fifties who exuded purpose and energy. Jason told Sarah that he saw her perform in Carnegie Hall when he was a graduate student. "I'll never forget your rendition of the Dvorak Concerto. You inspired me then and I still enjoy every CD you've ever made."

Sarah glowed at the compliment and said she had "high hopes" for the department now that Jason was the chair. "Thanks, Sarah. I sure hope I don't disappoint you, but I'll need your help. As much as I'd like to hear about your summer teaching at Tanglewood," Jason said, "I'm here on a more somber mission. I've already learned that the climate of our department is poor. I'd like your take on why things are in such bad shape and what we can do about it."

"I can tell you what the main problem is," Sarah responded, "but I sure don't know what to do about it." Sarah identified the problem as "faculty overload" and explained that the non-tenured performance faculty members were particularly overwhelmed. She told Jason that they lost a promising young pianist who quit in the middle of the year because of a nervous breakdown.

She continued, "Our department members have to meet the same criteria for tenure and promotion as other faculty members in the university. That means research as well as teaching and service. In addition, as you well know, performance faculty members are expected to win acclaim as performers. It's just too much. The university has turned down every tenure application submitted by our performance faculty in the past three years. It was even tough to get them departmental and college approval."

"It couldn't have always been that bad, Sarah," Jason said. "After all, we managed to get tenure and we're performers. What's happening here?"

"Ever since the new president came on board three years ago, the expectations for research have steadily increased," Sarah replied. "The president would just love for us to become a so-called 'Research One University.' We won't, of course, but in some ways it's even harder on our faculty to be a 'Wannabe' institution. Sorry Jason, I wish I could be more optimistic, but I just don't see a light at the end of this tunnel. It looks like a well to me and our young performance faculty members are stuck in the gunk at the bottom."

Jason's appointment with Bruno Cichowski, a leading light in the composition faculty, did not provide him with different information, but it did confirm what Harry and Sarah told him. Bruno agreed that there was bad feeling between the musicologists and the performance faculty and that the previous chairs exacerbated the antagonism. He also supported Sarah's analysis of the tenure rejection problem, but maintained that almost everyone in the department felt the sting of those rejections and everyone, without exception, was upset about the pianist's nervous breakdown.

In a distinctive eastern European accent, Bruno lamented, "It was so sad, Jason. Here was this lovely, talented young woman, destroying her career and her health trying to meet unrealistic expectations. It broke my heart. I wish I knew how to relieve the burden on our young colleagues, but I do not. What I do know is that we all want this to be the best music department in our state. I am convinced that we have both the talent and expertise to reach that goal. This is a balanced and exceptional faculty, but they don't know it. I truly believe that if our faculty members knew more about one another's work, they would come to respect each other. Please tell me if there's anything I can do to help you unite us. I wish you God speed and the very best of luck, Jason."

Jason thanked him for offering to help. As he was leaving Bruno's office, Jason said, "I'm going to need all the help and luck I can get, Bruno; you'll be hearing from me soon."

HEARING MORE BAD NEWS

Back in his office, Hannah said that Roy Burgess from Western had called three times. Roy was the music department chair at Jason's former institution and a good friend. When Jason got through to him, Roy said, "Hang on a minute, Jason. I've got to close the door."

"Hey, Roy, that sounds ominous. What's up?" Jason asked.

"Jason, I know how stressful starting as chair at a new university can be, but I thought I'd better call you on this right away. I just met with two of your top students. One is your first-chair violin and the other is your best cellist. They're here because they want to transfer out of your program. They have a boatload of complaints you need to know about."

Jason sounded weary when he replied, "Sure, Ray. Let me have it. My day couldn't get much worse, anyway."

"OK," Ray said, "but you'd better be sitting down. One of their biggest gripes is that your faculty members are at each other's throats. They were especially angry about a mid-term exam in their ethnomusicology class that the professor scheduled the same time as their chamber orchestra concert. I tried to assure them that this kind of thing happens everywhere because music departments have so many performances to schedule every semester. They told me, in no uncertain terms, that I didn't understand the problem. They insisted that the musicology professor deliberately caused the conflict because he hates Dr. Clark and wanted the students to come to the exam instead of the concert. They said that there were many more examples of how students were messed over because faculty members didn't get along or bother to communicate with one another. Both of them reported getting contradictory advice about courses they needed. These kids were really angry! And Jason, I hear they're not the first to bail out of your program. I know you well enough to know that you'll want to put a stop to it."

"Of course, I want to keep good students from leaving us, but it might take me more than a week," Jason replied. "I appreciate the call, Roy. I'd sure like the chance to meet these students, that is, if they're still in the area." Roy promised Jason that he'd let the two students know but warned that it might be too late.

Jason spent the rest of the week meeting as many department faculty and staff members as Hannah could fit into his schedule. To his chagrin, he heard other examples of students suffering because of poor coordination and communication in the department. The experience of the students Roy called about was not unique.

THE FRIDAY DEPARTMENT MEETING

Jason thought he was pretty well prepared for his first departmental meeting. He opened by announcing how proud he was to be one of their colleagues and how delighted he was to have been selected as chair. Just as he made this announcement, Hannah scurried in with a digital audio recorder. She apologized to Jason for interrupting and explained that every meeting in the department was recorded and transcribed for department members' review. This caused Jason to pause but he rejected his impulse to have Hannah remove the recorder immediately. "I'll have to handle this later," he thought.

Jason shifted gears from his rosy announcement and said that the dean told him that budget cuts were inevitable. "The dean warned that weaker departments are in danger of being phased out. We want our department to be as solid as it can be before the university does its program review. We should start preparing immediately. From my discussions with many of you, I've already heard that there are two issues that need immediate attention: (1) the difficulty new faculty members have in getting tenure and promotion; and (2) the rift between performance faculty members and musicologists. He asked if others agreed that these two problems were serious.

Jason saw a lot of nodding heads so he said, "I know I need more information to understand what's going on before we can work together on resolving these two problems. Would you be willing to discuss them now?" After an awkward moment of silence and fidgeting, one of the older faculty members suggested that discussions about these problems would be better handled in a smaller group. A tall, thin, young man jumped out of his seat and exploded, "It's easy for you to delay. It's much harder for those of us whose careers are on the line. Don't you get it? If I'm turned down for tenure this year, I don't know how I'll be able to support my family."

The ensuing "discussion" was not at all what Jason had hoped it would be. Other untenured faculty members supported their young colleague, arguing that it used to be easy to get tenure and promotion before music faculty were expected to publish. One of the senior musicologists shot back that the quality of journals for performance faculty was so poor he couldn't figure out why anyone would have trouble getting a few publications in their first five years. "How difficult can it be," he sneered, "to write an article comparing mouthpieces?" Things went down hill from there.

*TAKING IT ONE FRAME AT A TIME

Jason inherited a job that two previous chairs could not handle. His first department meeting ended in outright hostility. "I just started this job," he thought, "and already I'm out of control. I don't know what to do first. If I'm really honest with myself," Jason admitted, "I don't know what to do, period." At some time in their career, every dean and chair we know has confronted situations

---

*The previous analysis is based on the case of a new public school administrator described in Bolman and Deal, 2003, pp. 409–30.

like this. The effect is usually painful. Feeling overwhelmed and confused, their self-confidence is eroded. How can Jason escape this distressing fate?

Our advice to Jason is to sit down in a quiet place to reflect and reframe. He should systematically look at his situation one frame at a time, asking himself two questions: (1) what's going on? and (2) what are my options? Jason needs a better perspective—looking at the department from "the balcony" to see the whole picture (Bolman and Deal, 2003, p. 418). Reframing can provide a map of the department's terrain as well as the navigational tools to help Jason find his way (Bolman and Deal, 2003, p. 13).

After dinner on Friday night, Jason goes into his study and sits in front of his computer. He constructs a table he titles "Reframing North Central's Music Department." Underneath the title, he makes three columns: one for Frames, a second for What's Going On?, and, a third for What Options are Available? And then, he starts the hard thinking.

Structural Issues and Options

Everyone is into the "blame game," he thinks. Recalling a lesson from the structural frame, he realizes that people often blame one another when the real problems are with the system (Bolman and Deal, 2003, p. 419). Jason is frustrated with himself for making things worse, rather than better, at the meeting. "What the heck did I have in mind when I invited a conversation about those two touchy problems. I didn't really think through what I wanted. They weren't ready to have a civil discussion. I should have known better"

He stops, looks out the window, and shakes his head. "Wait a minute, I'm using a people-blaming explanation, too. Only, I'm blaming myself. Hey, I'm a 'people,' too. It's just so darn convenient to blame individuals. I need a different perspective. I've got to get back to the frames."

"So what structural problems does the department have?" he asks. "Well, for starters," Jason thinks, "there is poor coordination. It's all been left up to the department chair, and even a competent chair cannot do it alone. Maybe that's one of the reasons the previous two chairs failed so miserably." Jason realizes that there's no mechanism (e.g., an executive committee) in the department's structure to facilitate coordination. "Maybe I should see if Harry, Sarah, and Bruno would serve on an interim task force and work with me to address this problem. According to Hannah, they're all well-respected and in this department, respect is hard to come by. I'm going to call them tomorrow."

But, that's not going to address the problem of the untenured faculty members, he realizes. "Come on Jason," he tells himself, "this isn't the first time you've faced this problem. It's endemic in music departments." Jason recalls an impassioned speech about this very issue at the last National Association of

Music Education conference last May. The speaker argued that the "one size fits all" criteria for promotion and tenure are disastrous for performance faculty. He insisted that it simply wasn't possible to keep a respectable practice and performance schedule and, at the same time, become a productive scholar, excellent teacher, and responsible member of the department, college, and university. As Sarah said, the whole adds up to overwhelmingly too much!

Jason realizes that the speaker was talking about a structural problem: the criteria the university uses to evaluate faculty members are not aligned with the work performance faculty do. "We've got to make the formal policies work for us instead of against us," Jason thinks. He decides that one strategy is to formulate an alternative set of criteria to assess the performance dimension of a faculty member's work. The next step is to convince the whole department and the dean that the performance criteria should supplant the university's "scholarship" criteria. "But what criteria would work?" Jason wondered. "I've got some ideas but I'd better get some faculty members together and come up with a proposal. I'm going to make sure to include musicologists and composition faculty members as well as representatives of our performance faculty."

It is clear even from a few minutes reflection that the music department has major structural problems that have to be addressed. Jason thinks that the options he jotted down would begin to address these problems. But what to do about the toxic climate that makes it difficult to agree on anything? It doesn't sound like something a rational approach would easily fix. Jason decides to try another angle. He turns to the human resource frame for counsel.

Human Resources Issues and Options

"Our music department faculty members might be known for their inability to reach consensus," Jason thinks, "but they agree on one thing: this is an unhappy place to work." He saw plenty of evidence of open conflict and hostility in the meeting. "What's behind these bad feelings?" Jason asked. It would be convenient for him to believe that the previous chairs are solely to blame. If that were the case, he could "fix" the problem by being fair and competent. "I'm going to try hard to avoid the favoritism and mistakes of my predecessors," he thinks, "but that's not going to be enough to heal the department's psyche. Needy people do desperate things."

He shifts gears. "This is getting too depressing, I need to think through what a positive climate looks like. My last department had a healthy climate," Jason remembers. "What was it about my former department that is so different from this one? If I can pinpoint some of the differences, maybe I can come up with some ideas of what needs to be done here."

"In my last department, we respected and trusted each other. When there was a job to do, most of the time we cooperated with one another to get it done." Jason wondered if he was looking through rose-colored glasses. "Not everyone was lovey-dovey," he admitted. "I recall that we had some pretty heated debates. But when we had disagreements we were able to air them openly. That's the key," Jason realizes. "We talked with one another about everything. How can we learn to trust and respect each other if we don't communicate? How can we cooperate and reach consensus if we don't talk to one another from the gut? We can't!"

In the "What's Going On" column, he writes LACK OF COMMUNICA-TION in capital letters next to the Human Resources frame on his table. Then, he questions himself. "Is this too simple-minded? Remember Tom Lehr's old joke about communication? 'If two people can't communicate, the least they can do is shut up about it.' Very funny, but not very helpful," he thinks. "I might sound like I'm in Psych 101, but I really do believe that improving communication is crucial."

A good place to start, he resolves, is with his own behavior. Jason knows that the chair sets the tone of a department. He wants to model the kind of communication he'd like to see in the department. Jason vows that he will tell the truth no matter how tempting it might be to paint a more positive picture than the facts warrant. He is determined to communicate formally and informally with everyone in the department and to ask for input often.

Jason knows that he has a tendency to want to get the job done and get on with it. He's going to have to remind himself that if he tries to do everything, the faculty will not feel empowered. They won't bother participating. Asking questions is an effective way to engage others, only if they are listened to. "If I'm brutally honest with myself," Jason confesses, "I often 'listen to respond' instead of 'listening to comprehend' (Higgerson, 1996, pp. 54–57). I need to practice waiting a bit or asking another question before charging in. In fact, it's probably a good idea for me to listen to others' views before I state my own. My wife would love it if I could do this at home."

Recalling the way faculty members communicated with one another in the meeting, Jason decides that the department needs some ground rules for professional interaction. "We can't accomplish anything until we can be more sensitive to one another's needs. I'm going to draft an e-mail before our next meeting to ask for suggestions of ground rules for personal and professional interaction." Jason knows that coming up with a list is just the first step. Unless he enforces shared agreements uniformly, it won't matter what is on the list.

Checking over his notes from conversations with faculty members, Jason is struck by how many of them said that performance faculty members and musicologists avoid working together. Earlier in the week, Jason reviewed membership on departmental meetings. He noticed that either the musicologists or the performance faculty dominated the standing committees. The only group represented proportionally on committees was the composition faculty. He makes up his mind that future appointments will cut across these groups as well as mix faculty members of different professorial ranks. "People aren't going to learn to communicate," he tells himself, "if they don't have to."

"We've got good people here," Jason reassures himself, "but they don't seem to realize that they all belong in the same department. The musicologists and performance faculty act like they're competing with one another for power to get their way." With the internal review coming up, Jason knows that now is the time when the department's future depends upon good will and cooperative action. "I've got to be realistic here," Jason warns himself. "There is no way I could eliminate conflict in this department, even if I wanted to. Besides, it's healthy to have differing viewpoints. What I need to do is figure out how to deal with conflict so it doesn't do us in. I don't think the human resources frame can help me here. " Jason turns his attention to the political frame where handling power and conflict is a central theme.

Political Issues and Options

Jason thinks about the basic components of the political frame: enduring differences, scarce resources, conflict, and power (Bolman and Deal, 2003, pp. 421–22). "This sounds like a description of the music department," he laments. "If we can't move beyond our 'enduring differences,' our resources are going to become even scarcer. The dean is just waiting for an unfavorable evaluation of our department to cut our budget, if not our whole department."

"What's the first lesson of the political frame?" Jason asks himself. "Oh, I remember, now. The leader needs an agenda. I've got one and it's pretty simple: Number one, I want this department to survive. I don't think I'll have any disagreement on this one. And number two, I want us to provide an outstanding music education for all of our students. The key word here is "all." Focusing on survival and students, instead of our different programs or faculty interests, may help us shift attention from what divides us to what unites us. They're a beginning step to finding other common interests.

"I also need a strategy." Next to the "Political Frame," on his table, Jason jots down "recruit potential allies" under the column, "What Options Are Available?" "Wait a minute," he reconsiders, "I'm not even sure where everyone stands. I need to lay this thing out." On a new page, he labels three columns: "Allies," "Fence-Sitters," and "Opponents." At the top left of the page, he writes "High Power." At the bottom left, "Low Power." Jason takes about twenty minutes to create his political map. Reviewing it, he realizes that he needs more high-power allies. I don't know everybody yet, but I do know enough to see that there are too many powerful fence- sitters and opponents. I'd better start networking" (Bolman and Deal, 2003, pp. 422–23).

Sitting back for a minute to look at his chart, Jason thinks, "I'm getting somewhere, but it's still a little dismal. How can I help the faculty to see how great we could be if only we could work together? Where's the glue that can bind us together?" Jason asks. He's ready to start thinking about symbols and culture.

Symbolic Issues and Options

Jason stands up and stretches. Fortified with another cup of coffee, he reviews what he's learned about the department's culture. "Fragmented and hostile would be a succinct description," he thinks. "They're always running down one another, even to the dean. What can turn this around?" He remembers Hannah's observation that members of the two warring factions don't know anything about one another. "What was it Bruno said about this problem?" he asks. Rifling through his notes he finds Bruno's statement that performance faculty and musicologists would come to respect one another if they knew more about one another's work and values.

"That's it," he thinks, "I've got to provide more opportunities for faculty members to learn what makes one another tick." His mind starts racing. "How about a seminar/concert series? We could combine faculty seminars, where our musicologists discuss their research, followed immediately by concerts performed by faculty and students. I'd invite faculty members from music departments in other institutions, as well as our own. We might bring in alumni and students. Invite our dean, too. Make these seminar/concerts a big deal. At first, I'd probably need to issue personal invitations to every faculty member." Jason's mind is going a million miles an hour. "What about reserving the two front rows of our recital hall for faculty seating? I'll ask Hannah about hosting receptions for people to mingle as they munch on goodies afterwards."

Ideas keep pouring out. "Recognize faculty members' accomplishments at every opportunity," Jason thinks. "All our stories are negative. Let's hear some good news for a change. I'll start every faculty meeting with positive announcements about faculty and student successes. My weekly e-mail, Monday Morning Report, will highlight achievements. If we had a department newsletter, we could broadcast our accomplishments campus-wide."

Jason stops and takes a deep breath. "Wow!" he exclaims. "If I can come up with this many ideas in fifteen minutes, imagine what we could do thinking together? Besides, I'm willing to initiate the effort to unify our department, but I shouldn't be the sole author. I'm going to take Bruno up on his offer to help and see if he'd ask his friends in all three of our factions to brainstorm strategies for healing the rift and building a raft to move ahead with everyone aboard."

He catches himself. "It's fun to come up with strategies—ways to change our behavior that will make us stronger. But organizations are about feelings and attitudes, not only about actions. We need to ask ourselves some basic questions: Who are we? What are our values? What is most important to us? (Bolman and Deal, 2003, p. 424). We can all agree that creativity and discipline are essential elements of music education, but deep down we're caught between two versions of what we stand for.

Musicologists push for knowledge; performance faculty push for skills. We need both. That's what music departments should be about—educating the complete musician. Hey, I can see that on a banner over the entrance to our offices: "North Central Music Department: Preparing the Complete Musician." Jason makes a face. "Not very catchy," he thinks. "How about North Central Music Department: Knowing, Blowing, and Bowing?" Jason chuckles to himself and decides he wouldn't win many friends with that one. "Slogans aren't my strong suit and I'm getting a little bleary," he admits. "I'd better get my English-teacher wife to think about a good slogan. She'll come up with something jazzy."

Looking through the symbolic frame, Jason understands that a common set of values holds an organization's culture together. He makes a commitment to begin the process of reaching consensus on departmental values at the very next meeting. "I think I'll start by asking everyone why they got into music in the first place. I bet they'll be surprised at how similar their reasons are. Recalling how passionate we all felt about music when we started out might kindle some common core values. I know that this is going to be a long-term process, but it's sure a better use of meeting time than bickering."

Jason realizes that everything he's come up with so far means a lot of hard work for everyone. "We need to have some fun together, too. I know. I'll invite everyone over to our house for a beginning of the year potluck," he decides. "I'd like to have rituals and ceremonies throughout the year to bring faculty members together. If their students are involved, I bet faculty members will come. We could have parties after all the juries are completed each semester and, of course, a big bash for graduation. What else? I'm going to need Hannah's help. Maybe I could recruit a volunteer to serve as our 'social chair.'" Jason knows that he is perceived as a serious workaholic. "I've got to develop a 'lighter touch' if I want the department to be a fun place to work," he thinks. "Right now, though, I need to go to bed."

THE NEXT MORNING

The next morning Jason goes back over his notes. Is he making progress or just musing? He takes out the table he constructed last night (Table 7.1, Reframing North Central's Music Department). He looks at the list of what's going on and the list of his options in each of the four frames. "I think I'm beginning to get a handle on this. I realize that I'll probably stumble a lot, but at least I see a path. Just seeing a lot of options makes me breathe easier." He plans to spend the weekend on the phone talking with faculty members. "First, things, first though," he decides. "Honey, is it OK with you if we have the faculty over for a potluck next Friday night?"

Table 7.1. Reframing North Central's Music Department

Frame	What's going on?	What options are available?
Structural	Poor coordination; performance faculty turned down for tenure; evaluation criteria not aligned with work; responsibilities not shared.	Ask Harry, Sarah and Bruno to serve on interim task force examining structure; appoint faculty committee to develop a proposal for performance criteria; talk to dean
Human resources	LACK OF COMMUNICATION and civility; poor morale; rift between performance faculty and musicologists	Model good communication skills; get suggestions for ground rules; appoint balanced committees
Political	Conflict between rival groups and faculty ranks; resources threatened; too many high power opponents and fence sitters	Draw a political map; communicate agenda of survival and quality; recruit high power allies
Symbolic	Fragmented and hostile culture; negative news predominates; lack of rituals, ceremonies and social occasions	Propose seminar/concert series; tell positive news; brainstorm healing ideas (ask Bruno); create slogan; formulate common goals; host potluck

Chapter 8

Conclusion

Practice and Perseverance

Jason's analysis of the Music Department at North Central was built on his previous experience. The options he considered came from his own unique set of skills, intuition, and knowledge. A different department chair would raise other questions and select other choices. Reframing does not require mastery of a new body of knowledge. Leaders access what they already know when they engage in multiple-frame thinking. By systematically using all four frames to figure out what's going on, a manageable picture emerges. Deans and chairs stop feeling confused, overwhelmed, and powerless. Multiple-frame thinking generates a variety of options to consider (Bolman and Deal 2003, pp. 429–430).

We have spent most of our professional lives toiling in the ivory tower. We were initially attracted to academe because it gave us to the opportunity work with smart people, to learn, and to grow. We expected our leaders to be effective. Too often we found that they were not. We were inspired to write this book by the nagging question: "Why do smart deans and chairs do dumb things?" Since one of us is a former chair and dean who admits to doing a lot of "dumb things," this question was intensely personal. Our response is simple: deans and chairs, like leaders everywhere, rely on narrow views of their organizations that capture only part of the real picture. As a result, they miss out on a rich array of options available to them.

"Clueless" is an apt description of too many academic leaders. The problem is not that they (or we) are dumb. Despite the mean rumor that faculty members lose twenty I.Q. points when they become chairs, and thirty when they become deans, we know that most chairs and deans have plenty of smarts. But many lack an understanding of what they are facing and, therefore, of what remedies might work. We are convinced that learning how to reframe is the best defense against "cluelessness." Taken together, the frames can help deans and chairs accurately assess their problems and produce promising solutions. Let us briefly review the frames here (Bolman and Deal, 2003, Table 19.1. p. 400).

The metaphor for the structural frame is a *factory*. The structural frame stresses results and clarity. It focuses on the "architecture of the organization"—the roles, policies, and plans that shape and coordinate decisions. In a successful organization these are aligned with the work that is done and the organization's mission. The successful structural leader is an analyst and a good manager who understands how to make the organization function effectively.

The *family* is the unit closely identified with the human resources frame. This frame emphasizes the critical importance of understanding individuals and their needs. In an effective organization, as in a good family, members enjoy a caring, trusting environment. The leader is an effective caregiver and gives the folk he works with both roots and wings.

The political frame looks more like a *jungle* than a factory or family. It sees organizations as arenas where scarcity, conflict, power, and competition reign. Authority is assigned; power is up for grabs. Individuals use power to achieve special interests that may or may not support organizational goals. Politically astute leaders manage conflict and try to avoid dividing people in their organization into winners and losers.

The *temple* is a metaphor for the symbolic frame. People want more from their work than a paycheck. The symbolic frame accentuates meaning and value that are expressed through the organization's culture in sagas, stories, rituals, ceremonies, play, informal networks, and shared history. The symbolic leader's most important job is inspiration.

On first examination, factories, families, jungles, and temples don't look like they would have much in common. Yet, sometimes the frames overlap. For example, Jason was looking through the human resources lens when he decided the department needed "ground rules" to guide their interaction. But the symbolic or political perspective could also have suggested this strategy. A healthy organizational culture is characterized by civil, professional exchange. Ground rules are an effective strategy for managing conflict. Do not be concerned when similar pictures appear in two or more frames. And do not be fooled into thinking that overlaps allow you to take short cuts and ignore one of the frames.

Each of the frames has distinct advantages, and each of them has shortcomings. Bolman and Deal (2003) identify some of the limitations. The structural frame may "overestimate the power of authority and underestimate the authority of power." Adherents of the human resources frame can be "overly optimistic" about the potential of human beings to get along and their desire to improve. The political frame can lead to a "cynical self-fulfilling prophecy, reinforcing conflict and mistrust," and missing opportunities for rational dialogue and positive collaboration. The concepts of the symbolic frame "are elusive; effectiveness depends on the artistry of the user"(p. 332). The best way to steer around these potholes is to employ all four frames to set your direction.

A wise leader changes lenses when things don't make sense. All the frames are needed because each reveals different vantage points for examining a situation and generates different options. By way of review, *Reframing the Path to School Leadership,* by Bolman and Deal (2002; 4th edition forthcoming, 2009), provides a quick summary of general "leadership lessons" in each frame:

Political: Map the Terrain, Hone your Skills (pp. 51–53)

- Clarify your agenda.
- Build relationships and alliances.
- Soothe and learn from the opposition.
- Deal openly with differences.

Structural: Align the Structure with the Work (pp. 84–86).

- Clarify roles.
- Design groups for success.
- Shape a structure that fits.

Symbolic: Celebrate Values and Culture (pp. 104–05).

- Learn and celebrate the history.
- Diagnose the strength of the existing culture.
- Reinforce and celebrate the culture's strength.
- Mark transitions with ceremonies.

Human Resources: Build Relationships and Empower Yourself (pp. 66–67).

- Take the initiative to empower yourself and others.
- Open up communications—ask questions and tell the truth.
- Ask for feedback.
- Always remember that everyone (including you) brings human needs to the workplace.

These general strategies cannot be used as a checklist. We present them to inspire your thinking. They are no substitute for the options your own analysis will produce. The strength of reframing is that the more versatile your thinking, the more flexible your strategies. Remember the definition of multi-frame thinking: "the ability to think in several ways at the same time about the same thing" (Bolman and Deal, 2003, p. 433) Its product is useful knowledge. We cannot imagine a time when universities need useful knowledge more than in the present.

Today's deans and chairs are facing "a perfect storm" caused by a deluge of new students, coupled with rapidly decreasing revenues (Wadsworth, p. 35). Adding to this challenge is the fact that more of these students are "non-traditional" than ever before. The prospect for improved funding looks bleak. The severe recession has made the public more resistant to increased taxes and less generous with gifts.

At the same time that resources are dwindling and shared purpose is lagging, the clamor for greater accountability is accelerating. People are losing faith in higher education and demanding evidence that they are offering something of value to students and society. Championing standards and measurement has too often undercut the spirit that, historically, made colleges and universities special. Responsibility for the results of rigorous assessments of university programs is being dumped on deans and chairs, taking time away from other important aspects of their jobs.

Technology impacts deans and chairs in many ways and presents a new set of issues. They include: competition from on-line universities, fragmentation of knowledge and information overload, and the expectation that faculty members will practice more interactive teaching strategies. Exploding numbers of part-time faculty members threaten collegial governance, academic freedom, and job security. In short, middle management in universities today is not for "sissies."

Despite the challenges confronting deans and chairs today, we remain optimistic. More programs at the national, state. and campus level orient and support deans and chairs than ever before. The literature about higher education administration increases at an almost daily rate. Deans or chairs willing to devote even a few concentrated hours a week to study their positions can enhance their understanding and add to their repertoire. Because universities are embattled, they are becoming more willing to take risks, experiment, and innovate.

The main source of our optimism, however, is our experience with leaders who practice multi-frame thinking. The characters in our positive scenarios, Phil, Diane, Gary, Carol, and Jason are composites based on stories about real chairs and deans. We have found leaders in many different organizations all over the world enthusiastically receptive to reframing. It is liberating to discover that there is always more than one way to confront a problem. Applying the four frames to vexing situations elevates you above the confusion and adds to your palette of ideas. Multi-frame thinking can help you reach peak performance, but learning how to reframe takes practice and perseverance. At first, it may be slow and difficult to generate effective responses in every frame. But like any skill—playing golf, piloting a boat, or handling a leadership challenge—the more you practice, the easier, faster, and more natural it becomes. True learning comes from experience if you master the right lessons.

Bibliography

Anderson, M. *Imposters in the Temple: A Blueprint for Improving Higher Education in America.* Stanford, CA: Hoover Institution Press, 1996.

Argyris, C. and Schon, D. A. *Theory in Practice: Increasing Professional Effectiveness.* San Francisco: Jossey-Bass, 1974.

Atwell, R. H., and Green, M. F. "Resources: Management for *Colleges,* not Businesses," in Janice S. Green, Arthur Levine, and Associates, (eds.) *Opportunity in Adversity: How Colleges Can Succeed in Hard Times.* San Francisco: Jossey-Bass, 1985.

Balderston, F. E. *Managing Today's University: Strategies for Viability, Change and Excellence,* 3rd ed. San Francisco: Jossey-Bass, 1995.

Bennett, J. B. and Figuli, D. J. *Enhancing Departmental Leadership: The Roles of the Chairperson.* American Council on Education Series on Higher Education, Phoenix: The Oryx Press, 1993.

Berdahl, R. O. "State Involvement in Higher Education," in M. Peterson and L. A. Mets (eds.), *Key Resources on Higher Education Governance.* San Francisco: Jossey-Bass, 1987.

Berquist, W. H. *The Four Cultures of the Academy: Insights and Strategies for Improving Leadership in Collegiate Organizations.* San Francisco: Jossey-Bass, 1992.

Bolman, L. G. and Deal, T. E. *Reframing Organizations: Artistry, Choice and Leadership,* 3rd ed. San Francisco: Jossey-Bass, 2003.

Bolman, L. G. and Deal, T. E. *Reframing the Path to School Leadership, A Guide for Teachers and Principals.* Thousand Oaks, CA: Corwin Press, Inc., 2002; 4th edition forthcoming, 2009.

Bolman, L. G. and Deal, T. E. *The Wizard and the Warrior.* San Francisco: Jossey-Bass, 2006.

Bowen, L. (ed.) *The Wizards of Odds: Leadership Journeys of Education Deans.* Washington, DC: American Association of Colleges for Teacher Education, 1995.

Boyer, E. L. *Scholarship Reconsidered: Priorities of the Professoriate.* Princeton, NJ: The Carnegie Foundation for the Advancement of Teaching, 1990.

Branson, R. M. *Coping with Difficult People.* New York: Dell, 1981.

Breneman, D. W. and Taylor, A. L. (eds.) *Strategies for Promoting Excellence in a Time of Scarce Resources.* New Directions for Higher Education Series, No. 94. San Francisco: Jossey-Bass, Summer, 1996.

Brinkman, P. T. and Morgan, A. W. "Changing Fiscal Strategies for Planning," in M. W. Peterson, D. D. Dill, L. A. Mets, and Associates (eds.) *Planning and Management for a Changing Environment.* San Francisco: Jossey-Bass, 1997.

Buller, J. L. *The Essential Academic Dean, A Practical Guide to College Leadership.* San Francisco: Jossey-Bass, 2007.

Cameron, K. and Smart, J. "Maintaining Effectiveness amid Downsizing and Decline in Institutions of Higher Education." *Research in Higher Education* 39, no.1, 1998.

Chait, R. *The Question of Tenure.* Cambridge, MA: Harvard University Press, 2002.

Cheldelin, Sandra I. "Handling Resistance to Change," in Ann F. Lucas (ed.) *Leading Academic Change: Essential Roles for Department Chairs.* San Francisco: Jossey-Bass, 2000.

Clark, B. R. "The Organizational Saga in Higher Education," in J. V, Baldridge and T. E. Deal (eds.), *Managing Change in Educational Organizations.* Berkeley: McCutchan, 1975.

Clark, B. "University Transformations: Primary Pathways to University Autonomy and Achievement," in S. Brent (ed.), *The Future of the City of Intellect: The Changing American University.* Stanford, CA: Stanford University Press, 2002.

Conrad, C. F., Haworth, J. G., and Millar, S. B. *A Silent Success: Master's Education in the United States.* Baltimore: The Johns Hopkins University Press, 1993.

Deal, T. E. and Peterson, K. D. *The Leadership Paradox: Balancing Logic and Artistry in Schools.* San Francisco: Jossey-Bass, 1994.

Dickeson, R. C. *Prioritizng Academic Programs and Services.* San Francisco: Jossey-Bass, 1999.

Ehrenberg, R. G. *Governing Academia.* Ithaca, NY: Cornell University Press, 2004.

Farson, R. *Management of the Absurd: Paradoxes in Leadership.* New York: Simon and Schuster, 1996.

Fish, S. "When Bad Times Are Good," *The Chronicle of Higher Education,* January 10, 2003.

Fullan, M. *Change Forces: Probing the Depths of Educational Reform.* London: The Palmer Press, 1993.

Gunsalus, C. K. *The College Administrator's Survival Guide.* Cambridge, MA: Harvard University Press, 2006.

Guskin, A. E. and Marcy, M. B. "Pressures for Fundamental Reform: Creating a Viable Academic Future," in R. Diamond and B. E. Adam (eds.), *Field Guide to Academic Leadership.* San Francisco: Jossey-Bass, 2002.

Hansot, E. "Some functions of Humor in Organizations." Unpublished paper, Kenyon College, 1979.

Hartington, R. "Smart New Degrees Take Center Stage," *U.S. News and World Report,* 131, no. 11, 2002.

Hecht, I. W. D., Higgerson, M. L., Gmelch, W. H., and Tucker, A. *The Department Chair as Academic Leader.* American Council on Education Series on Higher Education, Phoenix AZ: Oryx Press, 1999.

Hersh, R. and Merrow, J. (eds.) *Declining by Degrees: Higher Education at Risk.* New York: Palgrave MacMillan, 2005.

Higgerson, M. L. *Communication Skills for Department Chairs.* Bolton, MA: Anker Publishing Company, Inc., 1996.

Higgerson, M. L. and Rehwaldt, S. S. *Complexities of Higher Education Administration Case Studies and Issues.* Bolton, MA: Anker, 1993.

Hossler, D. "Refinancing Public Universities: Student Enrollments, Incentive-Based Budgeting and Incremental Reviews," in E. P. St. John and M. D. Parsons (eds.), *Public Funding of Higher Education.* Baltimore: The Johns Hopkins University Press, 2004.

Karpiak, I. E. "Ghosts in a Wilderness: Problems and Priorities of Faculty at Mid-Career and Mid-Life," *The Canadian Journal of Higher Education* XXVI, 1996, pp 49–78.

Keller, G. "Planning, Decisions and Human Nature," *Planning for Higher Education* 26, no. 3, winter 1997–98.

Kotter, J. P. and Cohen, D. S. *The Heart of Change.* Boston: Harvard Business School Press, 2002.

Leaming, D. R. *Academic Leadership: A Practical Guide to Chairing the Department.*,Bolton, MA: Anker, 1998.

Leaming, D. R. "Academic Deans," in R. Diamond (ed.), *Field Guide to Academic Leadership.* San Francisco: Jossey-Bass, 2002.

Leslie, D. W. and Fretwell Jr., E. K. *Wise Moves in Hard Times: Creating & Managing Resilient Colleges & Universities.* San Francisco: Jossey-Bass, 1996.

Lohman, S. "Darwinian Medicine for the University," in R. G. Ehrenberg (ed.), *Governing Academia.* Ithaca, NY: Cornell University Press, 2004.

Lucas, A. E. and Associates. *Leading Academic Change, Essential Roles for Department Chairs.* San Francisco: Jossey-Bass, 2000.

Lucas, A. E. *Strengthening Departmental Leadership: A Team-Building Guide for Chairs in Colleges and Universities.* San Francisco: Jossey-Bass, 1994.

Lucas, Christopher J. *Crisis in the Academy: Rethinking Higher Education in America.* New York: St. Martin's Press, 1996.

March, J. G. and Olsen, J. (eds.). *Ambiguity and Choice in Organizations.* Bergan, Norway: Univeristesforlaget, 1976.

Martin, J. (pseudonym). *To Rise Above Principle: The Memoirs of an Unreconstructed Dean.* Urbana, IL: University of Illinois Press, 1988.

Massey, W. (ed.). *Resource Allocation in Higher Education.* Ann Arbor, MI: University of Michigan Press, 1996.

Mayhew, L. B. *Surviving the Eighties: Strategies and Procedures for Solving Fiscal and Enrollment Problems.* San Francisco: Jossey-Bass, 1979.

Montez, J. M., Wolverton, M., and Gmelch, W. H. "The Roles and Challenges of Deans," *Review of Higher Education* 26, no. 2, Winter 2003, pp. 24–66.

Morris, V. C. *Middle Management in Academe.* Urbana, IL: University of Illinois Press, 1981.

National Research Council. *Science Professionals Master's Education for a Competitive World.* Washington, DC: The National Academies Press, 2008.

Newton, R. "The Two Cultures of Academe: An Overlooked Planning Hurdle," *Planning in Higher Education* 21, no. 1, Fall 1992, pp. 8–14.

Peters, T. J. and Waterman, R. H. Jr. *In Search of Excellence: Lessons from America's Best-Run Companies.* New York: Harper and Row Publishers, 1982.

Plante, P. R. and Caret, R. L. *Myths and Realities of Academic Administration.* New York: American Council on Education, London: Collier MacMillan Publishers, 1990.

Rice, R. E. and Sorcinelli, M. D., "Can the Tenure Process Be Improved?" in R. Chait (ed.), *The Question of Tenure.* Cambridge, MA: Harvard University Press, 2002.

Riely, J. B. "Environments for Change," ERIC ED 911007, 1997.

Rojstaczer, S. *Gone for Good, Tales of University Life after the Golden Age.* Oxford: Oxford University Press, 1999.

Rosovsky, Henry. *The University: An Owner's Manual.* New York: W.W. Norton & Co, 1990.

Russo, Richard. *Straight Man.* New York: Vintage Books, 1997.

Seagren, A. T., Creswell, J. W., and Wheeler, D. W. "The Department Chair: New Roles, Responsibilities, and Challenges," *ERIC Clearinghouse on Higher Education*; Association for the study of Higher Education. Washington, DC: George Washington University, 1993.

Smith, P. *Killing the Spirit: Higher Education in America.* New York: Press, 1990.

Steeples, D. "So Now You Are a Dean: The First Hundred Days," in G. Allan (ed.), *The Resource Handbook for Deans.* Washington, DC: American Conference on Academic Deans, 1999.

Sutton, R. I. *The No Asshole Rule: Building a Civilized Workplace and Surviving One That Isn't.* New York: Warner Business Books, 2007.

Sykes, C. J. *PROF SCAM: Professors and the Demise of Higher Education.* New York: St. Martin's Press, 1988.

Tierney, W. G. "Mission and Vision Statements. An Essential First Step," in R. M. Diamond, and B. E. Adam (eds.), *Field Guide to Academic Leadership.* San Francisco: Jossey-Bass, 2002.

Trost, A. H. "Leadership in Flesh and Blood," in L. Atwater and R. Penn (eds.), *Military Leadership: Tradition and Future Trends.* Annapolis, MD: Naval Institute Press, 1989.

Tucker, A. *Chairing the Academic Department: Leadership among Peers.* Washington, DC: American Council on Education, 1981.

Tucker, A. and Bryan, R. A. *The Academic Dean: Dove, Dragon, and Diplomat.* New York: American Council on Education, MacMillan, 1988.

Wadsworth, D. "Ready or Not? Where the Public Stands on Higher Education Reform," in R. H. Hersh and J. Merrow (eds.), *Declining by Degrees: Higher Education at Risk.* New York: Palgrave MacMillan, 2005.

Wolverton, M. and Gmelch, W. H. *College Deans: Leading from Within.* American Council on Education Series on Higher Education. Westport, CT: Oryx Press, 2002.

Wolverton, M, Gmelch, W. H., Montez, J., and Niews, C. T. *The Changing Nature of the Academic Deanship.* ASHE-ERIC Higher and Adult Education Series 28, no. 1. San Francisco: Jossey-Bass, 2001.

Zusman, Ami. "Issues Facing Higher Education in the Twenty-first Century," in P. G., Artbach, R. O. Berdahl, and P. J. Gumport. (eds.), *American Higher Education in the Twenty-First Century: Social, Political and Economic Challenges.* Baltimore: The Johns Hopkins Press, 1999.

About the Authors

Susan Stavert Roper is a seasoned administrator with nineteen years in the roles of dean and department chair at Cal Poly State University in San Luis Obispo, California, and Southern Oregon University in Ashland, Oregon. Roper's work with colleague deans and chairs includes serving as one of three core staff member for the annual New Dean's Institute (sponsored by the American Association of Colleges for Teacher Education), chair of the California State University Deans of Education Association, member of the Board of Directors for the American Association of Colleges for Teacher Education and of the Advisory Board for the Journal of Teacher Education, and research associate with the National Network for Educational Renewal. Before her stints as a university administrator, she taught at the University of British Columbia and Stanford University. Roper received her Ph.D. from Stanford University in education and sociology (1971), an M.A. from Stanford in education (1968), and her B.A. in political science from the University of California, Berkeley (1963). In addition to her university positions, Roper has been a VISTA Volunteer, a public school teacher, a middle school vice-principal, and a Teacher Corps coordinator. She has published articles and presented papers about leadership, teacher education and evaluation, and partnerships between schools and universities.

Terrence E. Deal is retired from the Rossier School, University of Southern California, where he served as the Irving R. Melbo Clinical Professor. Before joining USC, he served on the faculties of the Stanford University Graduate School of Education, the Harvard Graduate School of Education, and Vanderbilt University's Peabody College of Education. He received his B.A. degree (1961) from LaVerne College in history, his M.A. (1966) from California

State University at Los Angeles in educational administration, and his Ph.D. degree (1972) from Stanford University in education and sociology. Deal has been a policeman, a pubic school teacher, high school principal, and district office administrator. His primary research interests are in organizational symbolism and change. He is the author of more than thirty books and a consultant to business, health care, military, educational, and religious organizations both in the United States and abroad. Deal lectures widely and teaches in a number of executive development programs.

Roper and Deal first met in 1967 at Stanford University where they were frightened students in Elizabeth Cohen's rigorous sociology of education class. They survived grad school and then both spent a few years working at Stanford's Center for Research and Development in Teaching. Although their careers have taken different paths in different places since then, they have continued to stay good friends and colleagues. One of their favorite past-times is telling one another outrageous stories of life in academe. They never run out of material. A few of these stories can be found in this book where they apply the concept of "reframing" to help deans and chairs make sense of their complex realities.

The authors appreciate hearing from readers and welcome comments, questions, suggestions, or accounts of experience from deans and chairs. Stories of failure are as welcome as stories of success. Readers can contact the authors at the following addresses:

Susan Stavert Roper
2711 Santa Barbara Ave
Cayucos, California 93430
sroper805@charter.net

Terry Deal
6625 Via Piedra
San Luis Obispo, California 93401
sucha@surfnetusa.com